Leyland Titan PD3

BUS MONOGRAPHS: 6

Leyland Titan PD3

Stewart J. Brown

LONDON

IAN ALLAN LTD

Contents

First published 1989

ISBN 0 7110 1639 9

Published by Ian Allan Ltd, Shepperton, Surrey; and printed by Ian Allan Printing Ltd at their works at Coombelands in Runnymede, England

Front cover:
Doncaster Transport PD3/4 with Roe bodywork.
Stewart J. Brown (SJB)

Back cover, top:
Southdown PD3 in Eastbourne. *SJB*

Back cover, bottom:
Western SMT Lowlander. *SJB*

Introduction

Double-deck buses of 30ft overall length were legally permitted in Britain before the relaxation of the regulations in 1956 which led to the introduction of the Leyland Titan PD3. There was only one drawback: they had to have three axles. Twin rear axles added weight, cost and complexity and, while the extra length allowed another 12 or 14 seats to be fitted, most operators steered clear of three axles.

Such models were, of course, available throughout the 1930s and the most common was the AEC Renown. Leyland offered a three-axle version of its TD-series Titan. This was the Titanic, an odd choice of name in view of the ill-fated liner of the same name which had sunk in 1912. Leyland's Titanic did not fail quite as spectacularly, but fail it did with only very small numbers entering service throughout the 1930s.

After World War 2 bus operators stayed with conventional two-axle double-deckers; no three-axle motor buses were offered for sale in postwar Britain until recent times, although three-axle trolleybuses were relatively common. The bus industry had been pressing the government to allow bigger buses and the maximum length for a two-axled double-decker was increased from 26ft to 27ft in 1950 and then again to 30ft in 1956. This was what the bus industry had been waiting for and this is where the PD3 story really begins.

This volume examines the rise and fall of the PD3 and of the Lowlander which was planned as a lowheight PD3 but which lacked the PD3's reliability and failed to make any significant impact on the market. Every British PSV customer for both models is illustrated and a complete list of chassis and customers is included.

As always, there are many people to thank for their assistance: the photographers, whose work is credited individually and my former colleagues at Leyland, Bob Smith and Alan Turner. John Aldridge provided valuable comments and additional material, notably the section *The PD3 in context*. Doug Jack's *The Leyland Bus* was a valuable source of reference and the PSV Circle kindly gave permission to quote from its records.

Stewart J. Brown
Withnell, 1988

Below:
Northern Counties exhibited this PD3 for Southdown at the 1966 Commercial Motor Show, by which time Southdown was the only operator buying fully-fronted, front-engined double-deckers. It was one of two fitted with Clayton Dewandre's Compass heating system which allowed the standard front-mounted radiator to be dispensed with. *SJB collection*

Above:
Yorkshire Woollen operated both PD3s and Lowlanders. On the right is a PD3A/1 with a Metro-Cammell body, and a Weymann-bodied LR7 pulling out from behind it. Both models had manual gearboxes. The rear end of a Lowlander can be seen on the left. This photograph was taken in Dewsbury in 1975. *A. J. Douglas*

Below:
The last home market PD-series Titan was ordered by Ramsbottom UDC and was delivered at the end of 1969, just after Ramsbottom had become part of the newly-formed Selnec PTE. It has East Lancs bodywork on a PD3/14 chassis. *R. Marshall*

The Quest for Bigger Buses

Over the years the harsh realities of economic life have caused bus operators to seek to maximise the carrying capacity of their vehicles. There have been two major legislative constraints on this — namely limitations on vehicle weights and sizes. These have been progressively relaxed as vehicle design has advanced, and it was one of these legislative relaxations which led to the development of the Leyland Titan PD3. From July 1956 the maximum permitted length of a two-axle double-deck bus in Britain was increased from 27ft to 30ft, and to its highly successful range of Titan PD2s Leyland added a stretched model — the Titan PD3.

This, however, was not Leyland's first foray into the 30ft-long double-deck bus business. Operators had been looking for bigger buses long before 1956. Edwardian trams could carry up to 70 seated passengers and, when these were being replaced by buses in many British towns in the 1930s, the new buses typically seated fewer than 56 — and with reduced standing capacity too. Bus use was expanding rapidly in the late 1920s and early 1930s; in some places buses were opening up new territory in the shape of suburban housing estates, while in others they were competing with existing train or tram routes.

Leyland's two-axle Titan TD1, introduced in 1927, played an important part in these developments, but was typically a 51-seater within its 26ft maximum length. To make it bigger required the addition of a third axle and thus was born the Titanic — an inauspicious name for an inauspicious model. The first Titanic was the TT1 which, like the TD1, had a six-cylinder, 6.8-litre, 90bhp Leyland petrol engine. Further Titanics followed, from the TT2 to the TT6, reflecting improvements being made to the successful companion range of prewar Titans. To say that Leyland's Titanic sank without trace would be to abuse poetic licence, but, outside London, three-axle double-deckers did not really catch on. They were bigger, slightly more complicated and more expensive to buy and to maintain than their two-axle counterparts. Traffic continued to grow, whatever the pressures on costs. More and more buses were being put on the roads, there was no shortage of crews to man them, and there was no shortage of fare-paying customers to ride on them. So the 30ft three-axle double-deck motorbus was essentially something of an oddity and Leyland built only 46 Titanics over an 11-year period. No three-axle double-deck motorbuses entered service in Britain after World War 2 until the advent of the rash of high-capacity 12m-long coaches in the early 1980s.

The PD3 was not a new model in the sense that Leyland's next double-decker, the Atlantean, was. It was in essence a long-wheelbase PD2 and as such was the final development of the Titan range which had been launched almost 30 years earlier. The original TD1 had been a petrol-engined double-deck chassis with a 16ft 6in wheelbase and typically carried around 51 passengers. It had been launched in 1927. At the end of 1931 it was succeeded by the TD2, which had a slightly bigger petrol engine (7.6 litres in place of 6.8 litre engine in the TD1). The TD3 which offered a choice of petrol or diesel engines, followed in 1933 and the TD4 which featured vacuum hydraulic brakes and a bigger clutch in 1935. The TD4 had a Leyland 8.6-litre diesel engine fitted as standard. It was followed in 1937 by the TD5, and in 1939 by the TD7 — each model having detail design improvements over its predecessor. The TD6 model was a type supplied only to Birmingham Corporation. The outbreak of war brought Titan production to a halt, with the last TD7s being delivered in 1942. A planned TD8 was never built.

The postwar Titan appeared on the roads of Britain early in 1946. This, the PD1, had a wheelbase 3in shorter than its TD-series predecessors at 16ft 3in. It also had a new engine, the 7.4-litre E181 which offered operators 100bhp at 1,800rpm, compared with 93bhp at 1,900rpm in the larger prewar unit. Versions of the PD1 stayed in production until 1951, although the more powerful PD2 with the bigger O.600 engine had been launched in 1947. The PD2 was the direct forebear of the PD3 and had a 9.8-litre engine (600cu in — hence its O.600 designation) which was rated at 125bhp at 1,800rpm. The constant-mesh gearbox of the PD1 was redesigned to offer synchromesh on the three top gears, making the PD2 a little bit easier to handle. Although it had the same wheelbase as the PD1, the chassis frame of the PD2 was of a new design.

Both the PD1 and the PD2 were extremely successful and were bought in large numbers by company and municipal operators throughout Britain. Export variants, the OPD1 and OPD2, ('O' for overseas) were sold in Australia, Ceylon, India, Spain and South and East Africa, to name but a few major markets.

From 1948 modified PD2s with low radiators, air brakes and preselector gearboxes were supplied to London Transport, forming the RTL and RTW classes. The RTWs were 8ft wide. Although overshadowed by AEC's success with the RT-series Regents, Leyland supplied 2,135 PD2s to London — a major achievement by any standards.

The wheelbase of the PD2 was increased by 2in to 16ft 5in in 1950 and stayed at this figure until production ceased in 1969. The PD2 was offered in two widths — 7ft 6in and 8ft — until 1962 when the narrower model was deleted, although a few were later built to special order. The PD2, like the PD1 before it, initially had a traditional exposed radiator. However an order from Midland Red in 1952 specified a full-width bonnet assembly to conceal the radiator and this new-look front, as it came to be known, was available as an option to all PD2 customers from 1953. Midland Red was reflecting current car practice in disguising the radiator although bus operators' views on the new look were divided. Some went whole-heartedly for the modern image which they perceived in the new-look front, while others stayed with traditional exposed radiators until they ceased buying Titans. Interestingly Leyland was the only manufacturer to retain this option right to the end of front-engined bus production. AEC, Daimler and Guy all abandoned exposed radiators fairly quickly, and by

Below:
The first long Titans were in fact Titanics with twin rear axles. This prototype TT1 had a 72-seat Leyland body. Note the petrol gauge, visible below the skirt to the rear of the access hole for the fuel filler. *British Commercial Vehicle Museum*

1960 all three were offering only their new-look fronts.

The next major PD2 development was the adoption of the new Pneumocyclic gearbox, developed by Leyland and Self-Changing Gears. This was a four-speed air-operated epicyclic gearbox which was coupled to a centrifugal clutch and eliminated the need for a clutch pedal, thus easing the driver's task in the increasingly heavy traffic encountered in city operation. The Pneumocyclic was Leyland's answer to the preselector gearboxes offered by AEC and Daimler and which accounted in part for these manufacturers' successes in gaining municipal fleet orders. It was only offered on air-braked chassis.

Thus by 1956 when the PD3 was about to appear on the scene Leyland's double-deck range comprised variations on the basic PD2 theme. It could be had with or without a new-look front; with air or vacuum brakes; in 7ft 6in or 8ft widths; and with the option of the Pneumocyclic gearbox. Only one single-deck model was listed for UK customers at this time — the Tiger Cub, a 30ft-long lightweight single-decker with a horizontal version of the Leyland O.350 engine mounted in mid-wheelbase. The Tiger Cub had been launched in 1952 and had quickly ousted the heavy O.600-engined Royal Tiger, although a few had continued to find their way to British buyers.

Leyland moved quickly with the PD3. The length relaxations were announced in July 1956 and the first PD3 was built (and bodied by Metro-Cammell) in time to be exhibited at the Earls Court Motor Show in September, in the livery of Potteries Motor Traction. Six models were offered:

Model	Design feature	Gearbox	Brakes
PD3/1	New-look front	Manual	Air
PD3/2	New-look front	Pneumocyclic	Air
PD3/3	New-look front	Manual	Vacuum
PD3/4	Exposed radiator	Manual	Air
PD3/5	Exposed radiator	Pneumocyclic	Air
PD3/6	Exposed radiator	Manual	Vacuum

All had the same chassis frame with 18ft 6in wheelbase, and all were 8ft wide. There were no 7ft 6in-wide PD3s. The frame was of conventional channel section construction and swept down between the axles to give a height of 2ft 4in above ground level. The wheels and tyres were the same as on the PD2 (11.00 × 20 on the front and twin 10.00 × 20 on the rear), as were the O.600 engine and the gearbox options. Manual models had Leyland's four-speed synchromesh while the semi-automatics had the epicyclic four-speed Pneumocyclic with its distinctive turret-mounted air-operated selector mechanism. The exposed radiator models had Leyland's traditionally styled grille while those with new-look fronts had the vertically-slatted grille with a shaped solid area at the top which had originally been designed to incorporate Midland Red's BMMO badge. All but the earliest PD3s had additional brake cooling grilles at the base of the new-look front, a feature which was also applied to PD2s from 1956.

Badging was minimal: the Leyland name at the top of the radiator on exposed-radiator models or, on those with new-look fronts, the word 'Leyland' on the filler flap and on a winged badge below it. Both carried the lettering 'Leyland Diesel' on the bonnet side. No alternative makes of engine were offered in Leyland buses at this time.

Apart from the lengthened wheelbase there were few other differences between the PD3 and the PD2. The rear axle was that used on the export OPD2 with a slightly different choice of ratios and of slightly heavier duty. The frame was fractionally deeper at 11$\frac{1}{16}$in against 11in on the PD2, and slightly thicker — $\frac{9}{32}$in, as on the OPD2, compared with $\frac{1}{4}$in on the PD2. The PD3 chassis was typically around 1cwt heavier than that of the PD2.

In 1960 the Midland Red-inspired new-look front of sheet metal was replaced by a new moulded glass fibre unit which had a grille similar to that used on contemporary Leyland and Albion trucks. The glass fibre bonnet cover was shaped to provide the driver with an improved view of the kerb. When this change was made the chassis code became PD3A; exposed radiator PD3s continued to be available. This modification also applied to the PD2 range and the glass fibre assembly became widely known as the St Helens front after its first customer.

The first PD3s were delivered to operators in 1957 and, surprisingly, the peak year for the PD3 in Britain was 1958, when almost 400 entered service. Thereafter sales of high-capacity Leylands were divided between the PD3 and the new rear-engined Atlantean. Atlantean sales immediately shot ahead of those of the PD3 and stayed there — except in 1961 when the British Electric Traction (BET) companies which had shown such whole-hearted commitment to the new rear-engined model paused to take stock of the situation in which they found themselves, and Atlantean sales momentarily dipped to half of their 1960 level. In the same year large orders from Glasgow Corporation and Ribble pushed British PD3 deliveries back over 300 for the first — and last — time since 1958.

The new bigger PD3 Titan obviously diverted some sales from its shorter PD2 stablemate. But from 1959 to 1968 total sales of both models in Britain were virtually identical, albeit with no clear annual pattern. PD2 deliveries were almost double those of PD3s in 1959, yet in 1961 the situation was reversed with the PD3 well ahead of the PD2. In its best year — 1958 — the PD3 accounted for 20% of all new double-deck bus deliveries in Britain, in a year in which Leyland had a 50% share of the double-deck market. But from 1963 when the Leyland Atlantean and Daimler Fleetline were battling for business the PD3's share of the market was typically around 5%.

The price differential between the PD3 and the PD2 was never very great. In 1958 the cheapest PD3 — the PD3/6 — was listed at £3,093 compared with £2,936 for the equivalent PD2, a mere 5% difference. Interestingly the price gap between the most expensive PD3 — the £3,484 PD3/2 — and the Atlantean at £3,680 was of around the same magnitude at 5.5%. Price differentials within the PD3 range in the late 1950s show that a new-look front cost £50 more than an exposed radiator; air brakes cost £70 more than vacuum brakes; and a semi-automatic gearbox cost £270 more than a manual one.

Above:
The use of single rear wheels allowed the chassis frame to be splayed out at the rear of the Titanic. Both axles were driven. *British Commercial Vehicle Museum*

The introduction in 1967 of a revised Pneumocyclic gearbox — the rationalised Pneumocyclic — brought about a change in PD3 type codes. Vacuum-braked models had been withdrawn in 1965 and the four remaining models became:

Left:
This PD3/1 in the fleet of Chieftain of Hamilton was one of the first chassis to be built and has a Midland Red-style front without the brake cooling grilles below the headlights. It had 73-seat Northern Counties bodywork and entered service in 1957. *R. Marshall*

Model	Design feature	Gearbox	Brakes
PD3/11	New-look front	Manual	Air
PD3A/12	New-look front	Pneumocyclic	Air
PD3/14	Exposed radiator	Manual	Air
PD3A/15	Exposed radiator	Pneumocyclic	Air

The 'A' suffix now indicated fitment of the rationalised Pneumocyclic gearbox rather than the St Helens-style front. The absence of a PD3/13 suggests a hint of superstition at Leyland Motors. There were no models with type codes PD3/7 to PD3/10.

The PD3 found a wide range of customers. Among the municipalities Leeds placed a big order — for 71 which were bought in 1958 for tram replacement — and this was followed by Glasgow which ordered 140 in 1960 for the same purpose. Leyland's slogan of 30 years earlier — 'Buy a Titan and bury a tram' — still held good. Leicester standardised on the PD3 and bought 117 between 1958 and 1968. A number of BET group companies also standardised on the PD3 — in particular Southdown, which bought 285 between 1957 and 1967. Ribble, another BET operator, bought 236 PD3s between 1957 and 1963. The PD3 was one of the standard Scottish Bus Group

Above:

The first PD3 to be completed was this PD3/2 with Pneumocyclic gearbox which was exhibited at the 1956 Commercial Motor Show and entered service with Potteries Motor Traction later that year. It had a 74-seat Metro-Cammell body with six-bay construction; all later PD3s with Metro-Cammell (and Weymann) bodies had five longer bays. It was posed for MCW's photographer before it was quite finished. Part of the wiring can be seen hanging loosely behind the driver's cab. *MCW*

double-deckers, invariably with lowbridge bodywork, and 298 were delivered up to 1961. A number of independents also bought the PD3, and in this small segment of the market some 70 were sold.

PD3s were, of course, sold outside Britain. In Northern Ireland the Ulster Transport Authority bought 142 between 1959 and 1963, while in Eire 152 were sold to Coras Iompair Eireann (CIE). Further afield the PD3 found a niche in South Africa, where a large fleet was built up by City Tramways in Cape Town. Unlike the PD2 range, in which there were uprated OPD2 models for overseas use, there were no OPD3s — the PD3 incorporated certain OPD2 features anyway. There were also no left-hand drive PD3s.

Specification

1962 model Leyland Titan PD3

Engine	Leyland O.600 9.8-litre (597cu in) six-cylinder diesel rated at 125bhp at 1,800rpm
Gearbox	(a) Leyland four-speed synchromesh with direct-drive top coupled to a 16¼in diameter clutch (b) Leyland four-speed semi-automatic Pneumocyclic with direct-drive top coupled to an 18in diameter fluid coupling with lock-up clutch
Rear axle	Underslung worm-drive with a choice of three ratios: 4.8, 5.4 or 6.25 to 1
Suspension	Conventional 4in-wide semi-elliptic leaf springs, 4ft 2in long on the front axle, 5ft 2in long on the rear
Brakes	Front 4in wide, rear 6in wide with total lining area of 577sq in. Choice of vacuum or air operation
Fuel tank	36gal capacity
Tyres	11.00 × 20 front, twin 10.00 × 20 rear
Electrics	24V (CAV or Simms) with 55A dc dynamo and 174A/hr CAV, Exide or Oldham battery
Instruments	Electric speedometer with mileage recorder; oil pressure gauge; oil pressure warning light; vacuum or air pressure gauge; steering-column-mounted horn and dip switch
Steering	Manual Marles cam-and-double-roller with 22in diameter steering wheel requiring 4¾ turns from lock to lock
Chassis weight	From 5 tons 1cwt 3qrs (PD3/6) to 5 tons 5cwt 3qrs (PD3A/2).

Front-end styles on PD3 PSVs in the British Isles

Midland Red-style new-look front	754
St Helens-style new-look front	460
Exposed radiator	433
Full-front bodywork with bodybuilder's own style of enclosed radiator	663
Total	2,310

Bodybuilders on PD3 PSVs in the British Isles

		Body layout			
		Highbridge		Lowbridge	
Builder	Quantity	Rear entrance	Forward entrance	Rear entrance	Forward entrance
Alexander	397		X	X	
Burlingham	144	X	X	X	
CIE	152	X			
East Lancs	193	X	X	X	
Glasgow Corporation	25		X		
Massey	49	X	X	X	
MCW group	510	X	X	X	
Neepsend	15		X		
Northern Counties	442	X	X	X	X
Park Royal	28	X			
Roe	174	X	X	X	
UTA	142		X		
Willowbrook	37	X	X		
Yeates	2	X			
Total	2,310				

Left and below left:
These views show a standard PD3/1 chassis with air brakes and synchromesh gearbox. The fuel tank was mounted well to the rear to optimise weight distribution. The simplicity of the PD-series Titan was one of the keys to its success and its longevity.
British Commercial Vehicle Museum

Right:
Stratford Blue, a subsidiary of Midland Red, opted for traditional exposed radiators on its first 30ft-long double-deckers, a trio of PD3/4s delivered in 1960. *G. R. Mills*

Below:
Leyland used a PMT vehicle to illustrate a 1958 advertisement for the PD3. This listed 17 operators which had ordered PD3s and said: 'Bus companies working the new front-entrance 30ft Titans are cashing in handsomely on bigger revenues and big operational savings on fast schedules. The wide margin of power of the 125hp diesel gives ample acceleration on stop-and-start routes and for speeded-up timetables. The adoption of the front entrance with doors under the control of the driver has speeded up loading, increased safety and freed the conductor of platform duties. And with the introduction of the centrifugal clutch in conjunction with the Pneumocyclic transmission (semi- or fully-automatic types), the fuel consumption is strictly comparable with that obtained with a conventional gearbox . . . and this with reduced fatigue and increased passenger comfort.'
Leyland

The big Titan's boost to bus profits

THE 30 FT.
Leyland 'TITAN'

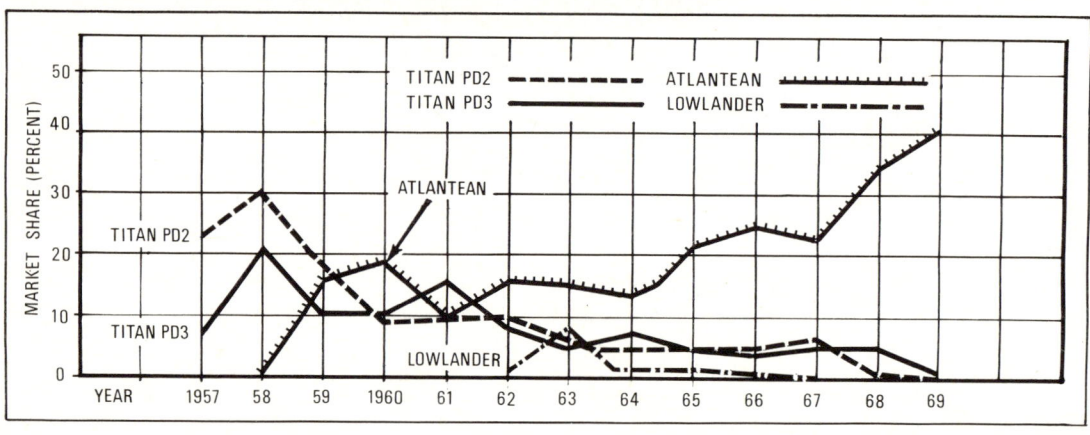

A PD3/6 chassis drawing.
Leyland

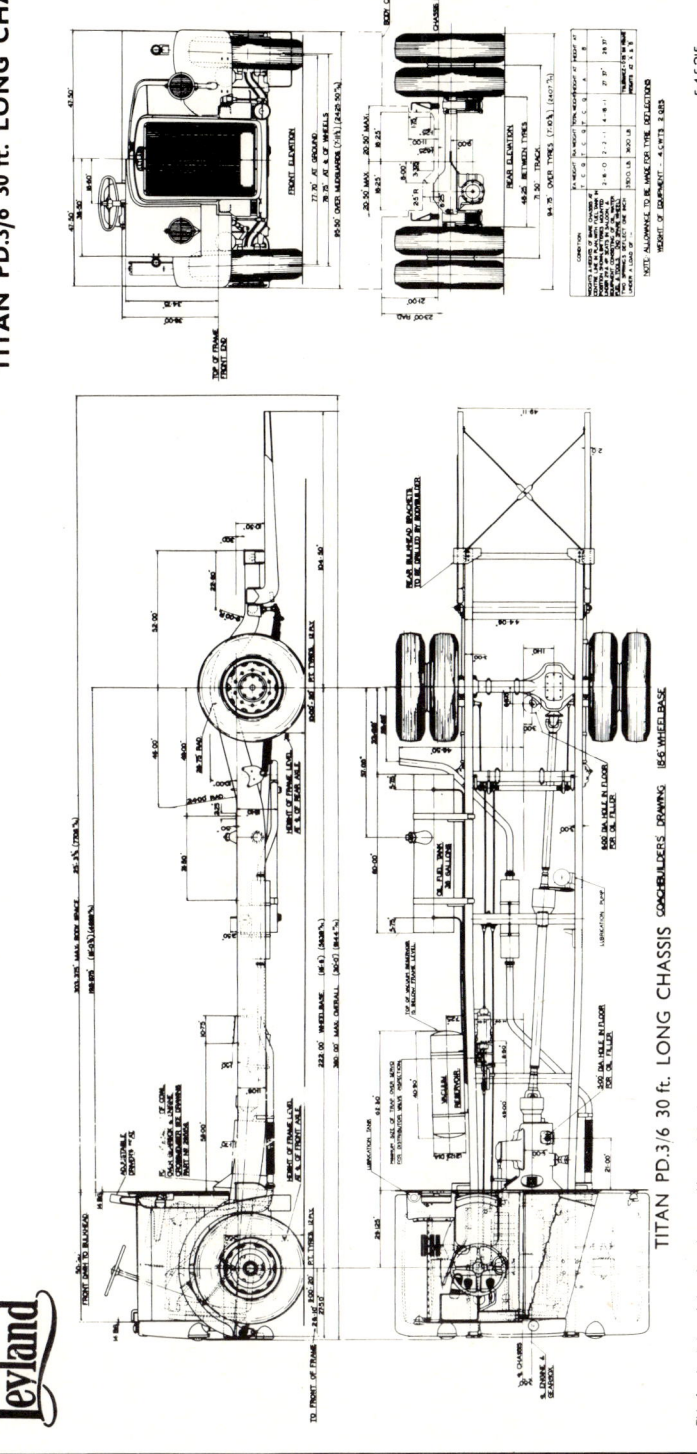

TITAN PD.3/6 30 ft. LONG CHASSIS

TITAN PD.3/6 30 ft. LONG CHASSIS COACHBUILDERS' DRAWING 18-6 WHEELBASE

This drawing is intended to show the general layout of the chassis and is liable to alteration without notice.
The latest large drawing will always be sent on application for Coachbuilders' use.

PRINTED IN ENGLAND

The PD3 in Context

John Aldridge

It is common to deprecate the contribution to the bus industry made by the Leyland Titan PD3. That is unfair and, indeed, a misreading of history, although the revolutionary rear-engined Leyland Atlantean, which would change the face of the bus industry, was already more than just an idea in the minds of Leyland's designers when the PD3 was introduced.

The PD3 was, indeed, a modest development of the PD2 and, some would say, not quite as durable or reliable. But when it was introduced it was ordered in quantity by a hard-pressed bus industry. Many undertakings continued to buy it, some spasmodically, others regularly, long after the Atlantean and other makes of rear-engined buses were widely used.

The demise of the front-engined double-decker — both PD3 and others — was brought about by the Bus Grant legislation. A major change in the law to permit one-man operation of suitable double-deckers (something most operators had never even dared hope for) meant a move away from not only forward-engined double-deckers such as the PD3, but also from recently-designed rear-engined single-deckers.

A few operators went on buying PD3s to the end. Such buses were generally used on the busiest crew-operated routes where there was as yet no thought of one-manning. Some of the late purchasers regarded the PD3 as the ultimate reliable bus. Geoffrey Hilditch in his book *A Further Look at Buses* refers to Leicester City Transport's PD3s with respect and appreciation. After quoting the maintenance records for a typical couple in the fleet (and both quite old) he says 'it is obvious . . . that these old buses coming as they do from a series of highly developed models, need very little maintenance. I would that some later

rear-engined machines exhibited such characteristics.'

It was to be expected that the PD3 would not be quite as reliable as the PD2, since it was using the same chassis components to carry a heavier unladen weight, and at busy times probably another eight or more passengers. Thus rear brake lining life was generally not quite so good, for example. But that kind of penalty was a small price to pay by hard-pressed operators. By the mid-1950s they were really feeling the pinch. Traffic had begun to melt away, aided by the growth of private motoring and the popularity of television. Costs were rising, and were hard to recoup: Traffic Commissioners scrutinised proposals for higher fares and often reduced the rises sought, yet one-man operation (of single-deckers) was not that common and often fought by the unions.

In such circumstances the revised Construction & Use Regulations in 1956 that permitted double-deckers to be 30ft long instead of 27ft were a godsend, quickly seized by operators. Even so, operators had to wait: the Ministry of Transport indicated at the end of 1955 that it proposed to allow 30ft from 1 July 1956, but it did not give precise detail on permitted weights until March 1956, so it was not till then that makers could get down to the detailed design of 30ft double-deckers.

The larger buses permitted a reduction in expensive rush-hour duplication, or perhaps a widening of headways on urban services from, say 10 to 12min, while retaining (or even improving) the passenger capacity per hour.

It must be remembered, too, that platform staff were becoming difficult to recruit, so a small reduction in their numbers was welcome.

Above:
A Blackpool PD3/11, one of 40 vehicles delivered in 1967-68 before Blackpool opted for one-man-operated single-deckers from 1969. *SJB*

Below:
The last 10 Yorkshire Traction Titans were PD3A/1s delivered in 1965 and had 73-seat Roe bodywork. The use of a sliding entrance door was by this time unusual. *M. R. Keeley*

Photofeature:
An A to Y of PD3s

What, you may ask, is an A to Y? It is one letter short of an A to Z, is the answer. The following pages illustrate, alphabetically by operator, examples of PD3s running for every bus operator in the British Isles which bought the type new, from AA Motor Services to Yorkshire Traction. A complete list of PD3 buyers appears on page 65, and of chassis numbers in Appendix 1.

The PD3 was a bus for big fleet operators — 80% of sales to operators in the British Isles were to fleets which bought 30 or more of the type, and included no fewer than eight which ordered over 100, albeit in some cases over a protracted period of time. These were Alexander of Falkirk, CIE, Glasgow Corporation, Leicester City Transport, Ribble, Southdown, the Ulster Transport Authority, and Western SMT. Southdown, with 285, was the biggest British user of the PD3. The PD3 also found its way into small fleets which needed big buses, with almost 20 independents buying PD3s in ones and twos.

The PD3, like the smaller PD2, lived through changing times. Initially it was challenged by the revolutionary Atlantean which over-shadowed it from the time of its launch. Then it saw further changes in legislation which allowed even bigger buses, with the arrival of 11m (36ft 1in) long single-deckers, typically capable of seating 53 passengers and able to replace early postwar double-deckers which seated only 56. The single-deck threat however was to come not from conventionally fully-seated buses, but from rear-engined standee models which could carry more than a conventional 30ft-long double-decker. First London, and then most other major British towns and cities, experimented with standee single-deckers during the 1960s. Leyland offered its customers the choice of the Panther or Panther Cub in this sector of the market. Neither model was particularly successful.

There was a reaction against early rear-engined single-deckers — from the passen-gers, who resented having to stand at peak periods, and from the operators who found that almost without exception they were unreliable. They had been introduced to effect cost savings by dispensing with the conductor (still an essential part of life in urban bus travel in the 1960s) and letting the driver collect the fares. But high operational costs and lost passenger goodwill often negated many of the savings being made. The legalisation of one-man-operated double-deckers in 1968 eased this particular problem by providing seats for everyone and by providing a slight improvement in vehicle reliability.

While the rear-engined double-deckers on offer from Leyland and Daimler in the early 1960s were more reliable than their single-deck counterparts, they still could not match the reliability of simple designs like the PD3 and its competitors from AEC, Daimler and Guy. This made many fleet engineers and general managers weigh up very carefully the benefits of the new designs being offered to them. A rear-engined double-decker certainly looked more modern and it offered a better entrance arrangement with a low step and the doorway under the driver's view. But if these benefits were to be gained at the cost of increased maintenance and reduced vehicle availability were they worth having? Those who thought not — often, but not always, in the smaller fleets — stuck with the tried and proven front-engined bus, albeit in decreasing numbers as the decade progressed and the reliability of the rear-engined designs improved.

The graph on page 14 shows how sales of Atlanteans were rising as sales of Titans declined. This decline was hastened in 1968 by the announcement of a financial incentive from the Government to encourage operators to buy new buses which were suitable for one-man operation. This new bus grant, initially equal to 25% of the purchase price of a new bus, was not something which operators could ignore. It effectively meant that if they were buying four buses they could get a fifth one free, to use consumer goods marketing-speak. They still had freedom to choose the manufacturer who would supply the chassis and the body, but to qualify for the grant the bus had to be of an approved layout — and the approved layouts did not include front-engined double-deckers with an entrance behind the front axle.

The PD3 and its counterparts from other makers were dying anyway. The new bus grant merely hastened their demise and a few — a very few — operators which had PD3s on order cancelled them. Brighton for example had ordered nine; they were cancelled and replaced by Atlanteans. Leicester similarly converted an order for 20 PD3s to Atlanteans.

The very last built-up Titan was a PD3 and it came off the production line in mid-1969, a few months after the last PD2. The last PD2 went to Darwen Corporation (it was a PD2A with St Helens-style front) while the last PD3, appropriately with traditional exposed radiator, was delivered to the newly-formed Selnec PTE at the end of 1969 but in the livery of Ramsbottom Urban District Council which had ordered it before the creation of the PTE. (A few later PD3 chassis kits were built for Ashok Leyland.) The rear-engined models had predictably won the battle for sales, although it had taken them 10 years to do so. The Titan name had been applied to Leyland double-deckers since 1927 — and was to be revived again for a more specialised and short-lived model in 1977. Total production of PD3s, the last of a long line of front-engined Titans, was 3,138.

Above:
Young of Ayr, a member of the AA Motor Services co-operative, was a confirmed Leyland buyer. This solitary PD3/1 with 69-seat Northern Counties body was delivered in 1960 and is seen here in Ayr when new. Subsequent double-deckers for Young were Atlanteans. R. Marshall

Below:
Accrington Corporation divided its chassis orders between Leyland and Guy, but with all bodywork being supplied by East Lancs. Its first two 30ft-long Titans arrived in 1962 and they were followed by three more in 1963. The first of these was a manual-gearbox PD3A/1, identical to the previous year's delivery, but the next two were Pneumocyclic PD3A/2s, one of which is seen here. P. Sykes

Above:
W. Alexander & Sons of Falkirk bought 102 PD3/3s, all of which had 67-seat Alexander lowbridge bodywork. They were delivered between 1958 and 1961 with the last 25 vehicles (which were in fact PD3A/3s) going to the newly-formed Midland and Northern companies. This 1960 vehicle is seen in Aberdeen.
SJB collection

Centre left:
The only PD3 bought new by a member of the Ayrshire A1 Service co-operative was this Alexander-bodied PD3/2. It had been built for stock by Millburn Motors, the Glasgow dealer, and was basically similar to contemporary Glasgow Corporation vehicles. The registration number of this bus was transferred to its replacement, a Volvo Citybus delivered in 1985. *A. J. Douglas*

Left:
New in 1968, this PD3/4 for Bedwas & Machen Urban District Council was its first new Leyland and its biggest bus ever, with 68 seats. This was also the last side-gangway lowbridge double-decker built and had bodywork by Massey Brothers of Wigan. *A. J. Douglas*

Above:
Blackpool Corporation switched from PD2s to PD3s in 1962 and standardised on the type until 1968. The first 20 PD3s had the original Midland Red-inspired new-look fronts and they were followed in 1964 by 10 PD3As. All 30 of these vehicles had 72-seat Metro-Cammell Orion bodywork with full-width cabs. *M. Fowler*

Below:
Bolton's last front-engined buses had full-width cabs. There were 17 of these PD3A/2s delivered in 1962 with bodies by East Lancs (on nine, including this bus) and Metro-Cammell. The asymmetric windscreen maximised the driver's view of the kerb, but could hardly be hailed as an attractive styling feature. This vehicle is seen leaving Bolton bus station when new. *R. Marshall*

Left and below left:
Bournemouth Corporation bought 30 PD3s between 1959 and 1963, the last 10 of which were PD3As. All had Weymann bodywork. The first 20 were 62-seat dual-doorway vehicles — a unique body layout on a PD3 — while the last 10 were conventional 68-seat forward-entrance buses. *R. Marshall/Weymann*

Below:
Bradford's indecision of 1967 — to buy Atlanteans, Fleetlines or Titans — continued in 1968 with repeat orders for all three models. The Titans were now PD3/12s instead of PD3A/2s and there were again 15 of them — but this time with bodywork by Alexander, a new supplier for Bradford. The 1967 buses had Neepsend bodies. These were the fleet's last front-engined buses and Alexander's last half-cab bodies for the UK.
Alan Millar

Above right:

Brighton Corporation standardised on the exposed radiator PD2 until 1965, by which time there were 54 in service. Its next new buses — and its last half-cab double-deckers — were five PD3/4s delivered in 1968. A further nine were on order but were cancelled and replaced by Atlanteans. The PD3s had 69-seat Metro-Cammell bodies and all were converted for one-man operation within a few months of delivery. (Double-deck OMO was legalised in 1968.) This 1969 view of the penultimate Brighton PD3 shows how the nearside front bulkhead was angled forward to give the driver space to collect fares. The built-up front wing was an unusual feature. Brighton's livery at this time was red and cream. *G. R. Mills*

Centre right:

Burnley, Colne & Nelson bought six PD3/6s with 73-seat East Lancs bodies — two in 1959 and four in 1961. These were the first forward-entrance double-deckers in the fleet. All subsequent BC&N Titans had forward entrances but were short PD2As with concealed radiators. *A. J. Douglas*

Right:

Bury Corporation's biggest single bus order was placed with Leyland for 25 PD3/6 Titans which were delivered in 1958-59. These had 73-seat Weymann Orion bodies which were unusual for a municipal fleet in that they had platform doors. They were Bury's last rear-entrance buses.
Ian Allan Library

Above right:
Caerphilly UDC standardised on Leylands from 1951 and on exposed-radiator PD3/4s for its double-deck fleet from 1960 to 1965. All had lowbridge 68-seat Massey bodywork. This was the eighth and last Caerphilly PD3 and it was fitted with platform doors which necessitated the provision of an emergency exit on the offside of the lower deck — on this bus the middle window was hinged.
R. L. Wilson

Centre right:
Leylands never featured prominently in the Cardiff fleet, but 24 Titans were purchased in the early 1960s and included six PD3A/1s with 70-seat East Lancs bodies. They were Cardiff's first 30ft-long double-deck motorbuses and were bought to replace three-axle trolleybuses. *G. R. Mills*

Right:
Carmichael's Highland Bus Service of Glenboig, Lanarkshire, bought this, the only new double-decker in its history, in 1962. It was the second of a pair of PD3/2s ordered for stock by Millburn Motors, Leyland's dealer in Glasgow, and had 72-seat bodywork by Alexander built to a similar specification as a batch for Glasgow Corporation — even down to the aperture behind the door for a route number display. This bus passed to Alexander (Midland) when the Carmichael business was sold in 1966 and ran until 1974.
SJB

24

Above left:
Central SMT was a big Leyland user serving industrial Lanarkshire. But although it bought large numbers of PD2s, it only purchased one solitary batch of 10 PD3s. These were delivered in 1957 and were based on the standard Scottish Bus Group PD3/3 chassis with manual gearbox and vacuum brakes. The 67-seat lowbridge bodywork was by Northern Counties. They were withdrawn in 1973. *SJB*

Centre left:
The chassis for this vehicle was built in 1957. It was only the third Pneumocyclic PD3/2 to be built (the first two had gone to PMT and Edinburgh Corporation) and was kept by Leyland for test and development work until being sold to Chieftain in 1959. Chieftain specified the forward-entrance Massey bodywork. The Chieftain business was sold to Central SMT in 1961 and this PD3 ran for Central until 1967.
R. Marshall

Left:
One of the biggest PD3 users was Coras Iompair Eireann (CIE). The standard CIE double-decker from 1959 to 1961 was the PD3/2 and 152 were bought from Leyland in kit form to be assembled in Dublin. CIE also built the seven-bay 74-seat bodywork whose ancestry could be traced back to prewar Leyland designs. This 1961 vehicle was 20 years old and nearing the end of its life when photographed in Dublin. *SJB*

Above:
Two PD3A/1s were purchased by County Motors of Lepton in 1964 to replace a pair of unsuccessful Guy Wulfrunians. They had Roe bodywork. This one was photographed in Wakefield when new.
G. R. Mills

Below:
Darwen Corporation only ran 30 buses and its biggest were five PD3A/1s delivered in 1964-65. All had 72-seat bodywork by East Lancs and were absorbed by the enlarged Blackburn fleet in 1974. This, the last of the five, is seen in the centre of Darwen in 1973. *M. Fowler*

Above:
The Delaine of Bourne purchased two PD3/1s which were fitted with highbridge bodies by Yeates of Loughborough. These were the only double-deck bodies built by Yeates, and were The Delaine's first 30ft-long double-deckers. They were photographed at Bourne in 1969. *G. R. Mills*

Centre right:
Doncaster Corporation's first forward-entrance double-deckers were four PD3/4s with 72-seat Roe bodies delivered in the winter of 1962-63. They were followed by six similar vehicles 12 months later, one of which is seen here when only a few months old. All 10 passed to the South Yorkshire PTE in 1974. *M. Fowler*

Below right:
Most of the East Midland Motor Services fleet was of Leyland manufacture when 10 PD3/4s were delivered in 1957-58. They had 67-seat Weymann bodywork which was unusual — for an English PD3 — in being of lowbridge layout. East Midland's next double-deckers were Atlanteans.
M. Fowler

Above:
Edinburgh standardised on the original style of Leyland new-look front, even after it had been superseded by the St Helens front from 1960. Indeed, Edinburgh even fitted Leyland-style fronts to other makes of chassis. All of Edinburgh's PD3s had forward-entrance Alexander bodywork and the last 25 were PD3A/2s which were delivered in 1966 and had their St Helens bonnet assemblies replaced by the Midland Red style — but made out of glass fibre instead of metal. These were Edinburgh's last half-cab buses. *M. R. Keeley*

Left and below left:
BET subsidiary Gateshead & District bought five PD3/5s with 73-seat Metro-Cammell bodies in 1958. They were the company's last front-engined buses. The vehicle in Gateshead's dark maroon livery contrasts with the 1973 view of a sister vehicle in NBC's version of the Tyneside PTE's yellow livery, complete with reflective number plates which somehow look inappropriate on an exposed radiator bus. *A. J. Douglas, R. L. Wilson*

Above:
Glasgow Corporation ordered 140 PD3/2s for tramway replacement. All had 72-seat bodywork by Alexander or were built to Alexander design by the Corporation in its own body shops. They entered service between 1960 and 1962 (along with 89 similar AEC Regent Vs) and featured Albion Titan badges as a gesture to local patriots. This was the first big Scottish order for forward-entrance double-deckers. *Harry Hay*

Below:
One of Glasgow's PD3s was in fact the first PD3A and was exhibited at the 1960 Commercial Motor Show. Unusually it carried a small Titan badge, barely visible in this picture but located just to the right of the registration plate. *SJB*

Above:
There were two batches of PD3/4s in the Halifax fleet with 72-seat forward entrance bodywork by Metro-Cammell (1959) or Weymann (1963). This is one of the eight with Metro-Cammell bodies; they were the first forward entrance double-deckers in the fleet. Halifax orders were generally divided between Leyland and AEC. *M. R. Keeley*

Below:
Harper Brothers of Heath Hayes ran three PD3As with Northern Counties rear entrance bodies with platform doors. New in 1968, they were the last rear entrance buses delivered to a British independent. Harper's business was taken over by Midland Red in 1974. *A. J. Douglas*

Above:
Haslingden Corporation ran a fleet of 15 buses — all Leylands and including 10 Titans — when it was merged with Rawtenstall Corporation to form the Rossendale Joint Transport Committee in April 1968. Haslingden's two newest buses were PD3/4s with 72-seat East Lancs bodies and were new in 1966 and 1967. They were the biggest buses ever owned by the Corporation. Haslingden's livery was blue and cream. *R. L. Wilson*

Below:
Huddersfield Corporation's first motorbuses were 24 Leyland Titan PD3A/2s with 70-seat Roe bodies, delivered between 1960 and 1962 to replace trolleybuses. They were also the Corporation's only Leylands: subsequent orders went to Daimler. The swooped red and cream livery was used to distinguish buses on former trolleybus routes (all of which were Corporation-operated) from those used on routes operated by the Huddersfield Joint Omnibus Committee and on which different fare scales were charged. *P. Sykes*

Above:

Hudson of Horncastle bought one PD3/3. It had bodywork by Roe and is seen here in Skegness in the summer of 1964 in Hudson's attractive cream and blue livery. It was withdrawn in 1972 and Hudson's business was taken over by Appleby of Conisholme two years later. *G. R. Mills*

Below:

The biggest buses on the Isle of Man in 1958 were a trio of PD3/3s newly delivered to Isle of Man Road Services which had previously bought PD2s. They had 73-seat Metro-Cammell Orion bodywork. They were followed by a further three PD3s in 1964 which were Road Services' last new double-deckers. This 1958 example is seen at Port Erin in 1964. *R. L. Wilson*

Top right:
James of Ammanford, a 35-vehicle BET subsidiary in South Wales, bought two PD3/4s with lowbridge Weymann bodywork. James had previously bought PD2s and from 1958 bought Atlanteans. The PD3s were delivered in 1957. The James fleet was absorbed by South Wales Transport in 1962 and the PD3s ran with their new owner until 1969. *R. Marshall*

Centre right:
After standardising on TD-series Titans in the 1930s and buying PD1 Titans in the late 1940s, Lancashire United Transport bought only one more batch of Leyland double-deckers which consisted of 14 PD3/4s with 73-seat Metro-Cammell bodies. They were delivered in 1958 and were bought to replace trolleybuses. They survived until 1970. *G. R. Mills*

Right:
An early bulk order for PD3s came from Leeds City Transport, which bought 71 PD3/5s with air brakes and Pneumocyclic gearboxes in 1958 for tramway replacement. They had 70-seat bodywork built locally by Roe. This was the biggest order for exposed radiator PD3s. *R. Marshall*

Above:
Leicester Corporation was the biggest English municipal user of PD3s, buying 117 between 1958 and 1967. All had new-look fronts and open-platform rear-entrance bodywork, and all but the final 20 had synchromesh gearboxes. The PD3/1s with Midland Red-style new-look fronts, of which there were 26, were delivered in 1958 and 1960 in this livery with a large area of maroon. Bodywork was by Park Royal, Willowbrook, East Lancs or, as shown here, Metro-Cammell. All were 74-seaters. This bus was new in 1958 and weighed 8¼ tons. The original PD3s replaced prewar three-axle AEC Renowns. *T. W. Moore*

Below:
Leicester's PD3A/1s, delivered from 1961, introduced a bright new livery to the fleet, with a minimum of dark red relief. These, too, were 74-seaters with a mixture of East Lancs, Park Royal and Metro-Cammell bodywork. A 1966 Park Royal-bodied example stands in front of two with Metro-Cammell bodies in this city centre view. *T. W. Moore*

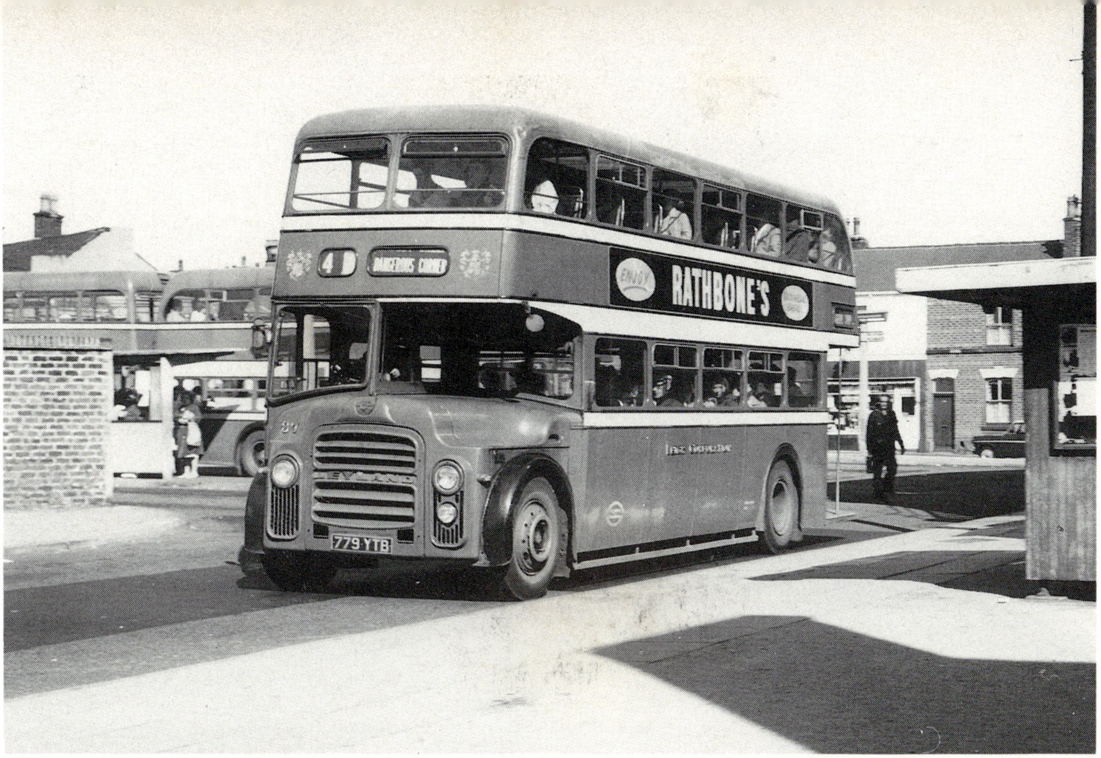

Above:
Leigh Corporation's two PD3A/1s delivered in 1962 were the fleet's last lowbridge buses and the last with rear entrances. The bodywork was by East Lancs. The combination of lowbridge bodywork and a PD3A chassis was unusual. All subsequent Leigh double-deckers were lowheight AEC Renowns.
R. Marshall

Centre left:
P. & O. Lloyd of Bagilt in North Wales owned one new PD3 which was fitted with Massey bodywork. It is seen in Holywell in 1969. Lloyd's livery was cream and red.
R. L. Wilson

Left:
Llynfi Motors of Maesteg in South Wales bought this solitary PD3/4 in 1958. It had Massey bodywork and was unusual for an independent operator at that time in that it was of forward-entrance layout. This bus served Llynfi for over 20 years. All subsequent Llynfi double-deckers were purchased secondhand. *M. Fowler*

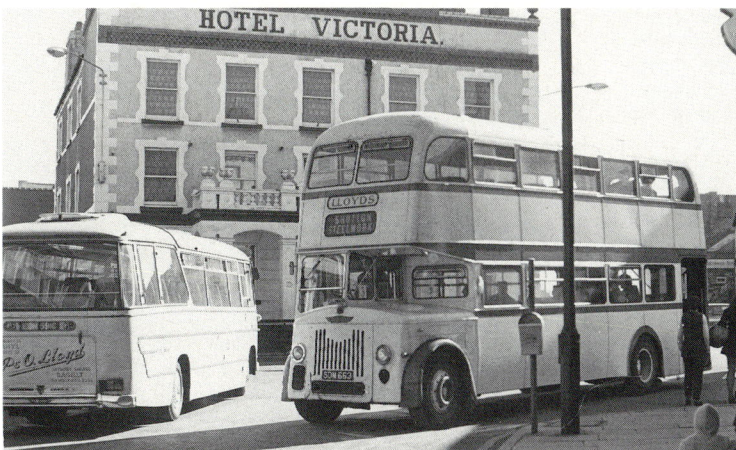

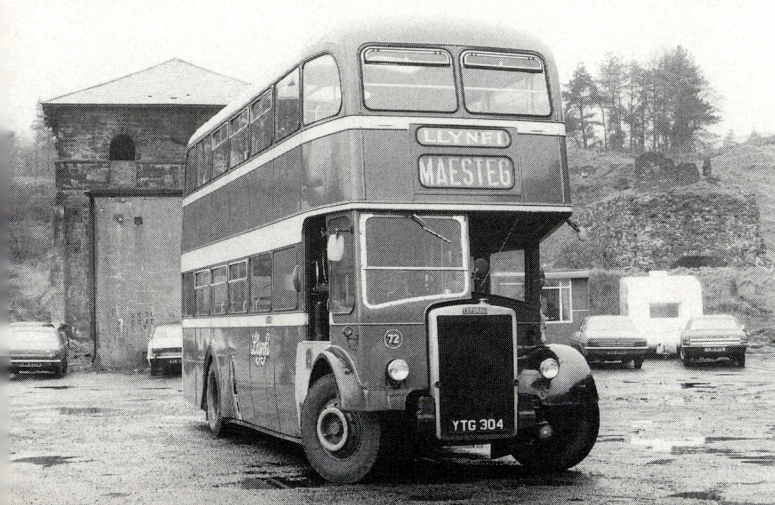

Below:
From 1955 Merthyr Tydfil Corporation standardised on Leylands and from 1958 to 1966 all new double-deckers were East Lancs-bodied PD3/4s. The first 21, delivered up to 1961, were of 73-seat rear entrance layout. This is one of the 1961 deliveries. Note the bonnet panel with the twin portholes, available as an option — at an advertised cost of £1 13s 3d (£1.66) in 1961 — and the proprietorial-looking conductor. After buying PD3s Merthyr Tydfil switched to single-deckers.
G. R. Mills

Left:

London Transport bought nine PD3s for use as support vehicles for the underground. They were PD3A/1s with manual gearboxes and had bodywork by Mann Egerton. Standard Routemaster-type trafficators were fitted.

Ian Allan Library

Above right:

The last front-engined buses for Newcastle Corporation were also its first 30ft-long motorbuses. There were 10 of these PD3/1s with 72-seat Weymann bodywork and they were new in 1957. All subsequent Newcastle 'deckers were Atlanteans. The PD3s were transferred to the Tyneside PTE in 1970 and survived in service until 1976-77. The absence of opening windows other than at the front was an unusual feature of these vehicles. This one was photographed at Tynemouth in the summer of 1966. *G. R. Mills*

Centre right:

Twenty PD3/4s were delivered to Northern General in 1958. They had Metro-Cammell 72-seat bodywork and were Northern General's last Titans: the next double-deck order specified rear-engined Atlanteans. Although carrying Northern fleetnames this vehicle was one of a pair which were loaned to Gateshead & District in 1970 and were repainted in Gateshead green and cream. The last of these buses was withdrawn in 1976.

R. L. Wilson

Right:

OK Motor Services of Bishop Auckland bought one new PD3/6. It had Roe rear entrance bodywork with platform doors. OK built up a fleet of secondhand PD3s in the 1970s. *A. J. Douglas*

Above:

This Oldham Corporation PD3/5 epitomises traditional municipal bus operation. The handsome Roe bodywork wears the modern livery layout well and this smart bus almost invites you to travel on it. It was one of 10 delivered in 1964 and they represented a watershed in Oldham's buying policy. **They were the last half-cab buses to be bought, but they were also the first double-deckers with forward entrances: Oldham had previously bought open-platform PD2s (but with new-look fronts). Subsequent purchases were Atlanteans. Note the two translucent panels in the roof — luxury indeed!** *Ian Allan Library*

Above right:
An odd vehicle in the PMT fleet was this solitary PD3/3. It had been ordered by Baxter of Hanley, whose business was acquired by PMT at the end of 1958, and was delivered to PMT, in PMT livery, in 1960. Willowbrook 73-seat forward-entrance bodywork was fitted. *A. Moyes*

Right:
From 1952 to 1982 all of Portsmouth's new buses were Leylands. PD2 Titans were purchased until 1958 and were followed by five PD3/6s in 1959. They had 64-seat Metro-Cammell bodies which were quickly upseated to 70. They were Portsmouth's last front-engined buses. The next double-deckers were Atlanteans. *A. D. Broughall*

Below right:
Preston Corporation's first 30ft-long 'deckers were seven Pneumocyclic PD3/5s with 72-seat Metro-Cammell bodywork. The first is seen when new — in 1958 — in Preston's drab dark maroon livery. A further seven exposed-radiator PD3/4s with manual gearboxes were delivered in 1961. They had similar bodywork.
Ian Allan Library

Left:
PMT bought the first PD3 to be completed and it was followed by a batch of 15 PD3/4s with manual gearboxes. These had forward-entrance Metro-Cammell Aurora bodywork with the unusually low seating capacity of 68 and were delivered in 1957. They were PMT's first forward-entrance 'deckers. *MCW*

Above:
Ramsbottom UDC's 12-vehicle fleet was taken over by the Selnec PTE in November 1969, at which time no fewer than eight of its vehicles were PD3s, all with 73-seat East Lancs forward-entrance bodywork. Delivered between 1965 and 1969 they comprised two PD3A/1s with St Helens fronts and four PD3/4s plus two PD3/14s with exposed radiators. All had manual gearboxes. This PD3/4 was new in 1967 and is seen at Ramsbottom station in 1968. *A. C. Turner-Bishop*

Below:
Between 1964 and 1966 Rawtenstall Corporation bought 12 PD3/4s. These were fitted with 73-seat forward-entrance East Lancs bodies and were Rawtenstall's last new buses. They were the last of a long line of Titans stretching back to the original TD1. Rawtenstall merged with Haslingden to form the Rossendale fleet in 1968 — the two concerns had been run by the same manager for many years. *P. J. Relf*

Above:
Ribble Motor Services, a staunch Leyland user, was one of the biggest buyers of the PD3 — 236 entered service between 1957 and 1963 at a time when Ribble's orders were divided between the conventional Titan and the advanced Atlantean. All of Ribble's Titans were PD3/5s and all had full-fronted bodywork, a feature seen previously on Ribble Titan coaches, but not on buses. The first 105 had 72-seat bodywork by local builder Burlingham of Blackpool, a company better known for its coach bodywork. Ribble was the first BET company to abandon rear-entrance bodywork with a large order for the new (or rediscovered) forward entrance layout. This bus is seen in Manchester in 1960. *R. L. Wilson*

Right:
The forward-entrance layout was sufficiently novel in 1957 to merit close examination. The contemporary caption in *Passenger Transport* mentioned the shallow steps and adequate grab rails.
Ian Allan Library

Above:

Scout Motor Services of Preston bought three PD3/1s in 1959. These had 72-seat Burlingham bodies generally similar to those on Ribble's PD3s but with conventional half-cabs. Scout was taken over by Ribble in 1962 and these buses received Ribble's maroon livery but with Scout fleetnames.
R. Marshall

Below:

Thirty PD3/1s were bought by Sheffield Corporation in 1959. They were the fleet's last Titans (but not the last half-cabs — they were followed by some AEC Regent Vs). Roe built the 69-seat rear-entrance bodies on these vehicles.
G. R. Mills

Above:

Nottingham independent Skill's was an infrequent buyer of new double-deckers. The last were two PD3s with forward-entrance Metro-Cammell bodies. Note the unusual location for the side destination screen towards the rear of the vehicle. *SJB*

Below:

Southdown was the biggest British customer for the PD3, buying 285 between 1957 and 1967. All had distinctive fully-fronted forward entrance 69-seat highbridge bodywork by Northern Counties. One batch of 40, delivered in 1961, were PD3/5s with Pneumocyclic gearboxes but all of the others were manual gearbox PD3/4s. This is a 1965 PD3/4 in Hove in 1974. It is in Southdown's traditional bright green livery but with NBC-style fleetname. *M. Fowler*

Above:
In 1964-65 a batch of 30 convertible open-toppers was delivered to Southdown and many of these were to give over 20 years of service. This view shows a topless example loading in Eastbourne for a trip to Beachy Head in the summer of 1970.
Alan Millar

Below:
The modernised Northern Counties body on the last 24 Titans delivered in 1967 had panoramic side windows. This vehicle is seen operating in Brighton in 1979. The attempt at modernity had not really succeeded. *S. J. Butler*

Above:
Southend Corporation bought half a dozen PD3/6s in 1958 — it had previously been buying PD2s — and these had lowbridge Massey bodywork with 68 seats. *Ian Allan Library*

Below:
The second and last pair of PD3s for South Notts was delivered in 1961 and 1962 and had Northern Counties bodywork which was unusual in being of forward-entrance lowbridge layout. This PD3/4 was delivered in 1962 and had 65 seats. Note the unusual position of the door, set back about 18in from the front bulkhead, and the small side destination screen. This bus ran for 20 years, outlasting the Lowlanders which followed it. *SJB*

Above:
South Yorkshire Motors' only PD3s were a pair of PD3/1s with lowbridge Roe bodywork fitted with platform doors. Subsequent South Yorkshire double-deckers were Atlanteans and then Fleetlines. *Roe*

Below:
The conservative Stockport Corporation fleet did not receive any 30ft-long double-deckers until 1968 and even then they were exposed radiator PD3/14s with manual gearboxes and open-platform East Lancs 70-seat bodies. They were followed by further similar vehicles in 1969, along with six with forward-entrance bodies. These fine vehicles were splendidly anachronistic.
R. L. Wilson

Above:
For its last eight Titans, Stratford Blue specified concealed radiators and Willowbrook bodies. There were eight of these PD3A/1s delivered in 1963 (six) and 1966 (two). All were sold by Midland Red in 1972, joining the Isle of Man Road Services fleet. *M. R. Keeley*

Below:
While Northern General and its other associates were buying Metro-Cammell-bodied PD3s, Sunderland District opted for Burlingham bodywork. There were 13 of these PD3/4s in the Sunderland District fleet and they were the last traditional half-cab buses to be bought by them. They were new in 1958 and ran until the early 1970s. *G. R. Mills*

Above:
Trent's last half-cab buses were 22 PD3/4s which were new in 1958; like many other BET companies Trent switched to rear-engined Atlanteans in the late 1950s. All of Trent's PD3s had Willowbrook 73-seat bodywork and this vehicle had an early example of illuminated exterior advertising, a short-lived feature on some double-deckers in the early 1960s. *Ian Allan Library*

Below:
Two PD3s were delivered to Staffordshire independent Turner of Brown Edge. This PD3/1 was new in 1959 and had 72-seat forward-entrance Massey bodywork. It ran for Turner until 1970 and then saw further service with another PD3-buying independent, Weardale Motor Services. *G. R. Mills*

Above:
Tynemouth & District was not a big Titan user — a batch of TD5s in 1938, some PD2s in 1957, and then a dozen PD3/4s in 1958. The PD3s had 73-seat Metro-Cammell Orion bodies. As with many other BET fleets subsequent double-deck purchases were rear-engined. *G. R. Mills*

Below:
Tyneside, a company connected with Tynemouth & District, received three PD3/4s at the same time. This one is seen in 1966 with patriotic advertising on the side. It was new in 1958; Tyneside's next new buses were a trio of Atlanteans in 1964. *R. Marshall*

Above left:
The Ulster Transport Authority, the forerunner of Ulsterbus, was a big Titan user and bought no fewer than 142 PD3s. These had UTA-built bodywork based on Metro-Cammell designs and with full-width cabs. This one is seen at Coleraine station in 1964. *R. C. Ludgate*

Left:
An UTA PD3 body under construction at Duncrue Street works, Belfast.
R. C. Ludgate

Below:
The last of seven Wallace Arnold Titans was delivered in 1966. This vehicle in the Farsley Omnibus Co fleet was photographed at Pudsey bus station in March 1968, shortly before the service (but not the vehicle) was taken over by Leeds City Transport.
M. Fowler

Above right:
An Alexander-bodied bus was a most unusual purchase for an English independent when this PD3 was delivered to Weardale Motor Services in 1959. The body was similar to five being built for Edinburgh Corporation at the same time; later versions of this body had a less severe rear dome.
A. J. Douglas

Centre right:
The biggest Scottish customer for the PD3 was Western SMT, with a total of 186 PD3/3s being placed in service between 1957 and 1961. All had 67-seat lowbridge bodywork which on this 1958 example was by Northern Counties. It was photographed in Kilmarnock in 1974. *M. R. Keeley*

Right:
Wigan Corporation bought PD3s from 1959 to 1961 and then reverted to the smaller PD2 model until 1967. Its body orders were divided between the town's two coachbuilders, Massey Bros and Northern Counties. The 70-seat Northern Counties body on this 1960 PD3/2 shared a number of features with the well known Southdown PD3s including the short central bay and the radiused side window at the rear of the lower saloon. *R. L. Wilson*

Above:

From 1955 to 1961 Yorkshire Traction rebuilt Tigers as double-deckers as an alternative to purchasing new vehicles. After buying one batch of Atlanteans in 1959 Yorkshire Traction turned to PD3A/1 Titans for new purchases and built up a fleet of 45 between 1961 and 1966. The early vehicles — this is the first — had Northern Counties 73-seat bodywork with equal-length bays instead of having a short centre bay as specified by Southdown and Wigan. Note the unused illuminated advertisement in this view taken when the bus was new. *R. L. Wilson*

Below:

Yorkshire Woollen was unusual among BET companies in that it had been buying 30ft-long AEC Regent Vs for four years when in 1962 it received a batch of nine PD3A/1s. Metro-Cammell, which had bodied most of the Regents, built the 70-seat bodywork for the Titans. Yorkshire Woollen's drab overall red livery matches the Manchester weather in this April 1963 view. *R. L. Wilson*

Top right:
One of the biggest export markets was South Africa, where the City Tramways group standardised on PD3s. All had fully-fronted forward-entrance bodywork by Bus Bodies (South Africa) of Port Elizabeth. The front incorporated the radiator grille panel and the brake cooling grilles of the standard PD3A. This bus is seen operating in Cape Town. *SJB*

Above right:
The first double-deckers in Mauritius were 10 PD3A/2s with locally-built six-bay bodywork which used Metsec framing. They were delivered in 1962. Note the Leyland name above the destination screen and the imitation bumper fitted to the front. *Leyland*

Right:
The first — and for many years the only — double-decker in Indonesia was this Metro-Cammell-bodied PD3/11 which was built in 1968 to a broadly similar specification to vehicles then being delivered to Blackpool Corporation. It had a substantial front bumper and a width marker mounted on the nearside wing. Indonesia later bought Atlanteans. *SJB collection*

Rebuilds

Three operators introduced what might be termed quasi-PD3s into their fleets. The first was Preston Corporation which embarked on what was an ambitious rebuilding programme for a small municipal fleet and involved lengthening the Leyland bodywork on a PD2 and fitting the vehicle with new PD3 chassis frames purchased from Leyland. The bodywork was also converted from rear-entrance to forward-entrance and, on four vehicles, from lowbridge to highbridge. The first such rebuild appeared in 1959 and was followed by a further seven in the following seven years. These vehicles were 7ft 6in wide.

The next was Alexander of Falkirk which in 1961 bought 17 PD3 chassis frames into which it fitted the units from a fleet of nine-year-old Tiger OPS2 coaches. (The OPS2s were in turn fitted with the units from PS1 Tigers which were being scrapped.) These vehicles were fitted with new 67-seat Alexander lowbridge bodywork and ran for 16 years.

Finally CIE added 26 PD3A rebuilds to its fleet in 1964-65. These had new frames and, like the Alexander vehicles, utilised parts from withdrawn Tigers. They had vacuum brakes and synchromesh gearboxes which effectively made them PD3A/3s, although CIE designated them PD3A/6s. (While, ironically, Alexander's rebuilds were to PD3/6 standard but were known by the company as PD3/3Cs.) The bodywork on the CIE vehicles was built in Dundalk by Commercial Road Vehicles on Park Royal frames.

Left:
Preston Corporation's rebuilds were extensive. The vehicles were lengthened and had their Leyland Farington bodies converted to forward entrance layout — and in this instance from lowbridge to highbridge too. *Ian Allan Library*

Above:
Alexander fitted new 67-seat lowbridge bodywork to its rebuilds, classed by the company as PD3/3C, although they were in effect PD3/6s. They entered service in the early part of 1961 and survived with Alexander (Midland) until 1976, lasting as long as factory-built PD3s bought at the same time. They were SBG's last new exposed-radiator buses and its only exposed-radiator PD3s. *SJB*

Below:
CIE operated 26 PD3 rebuilds using new frames and parts from old Tigers. They had St Helens-style fronts and were classed as PD3A/6s by CIE. The Commercial Road Vehicles 74-seat highbridge bodywork was quite obviously of Park Royal descent with its uncompromising flat sides. *SJB*

Above and below:

The most extensive rebuild of all was carried out by Northern General. This accident-damaged PD3 was rebuilt as a semi-forward-control double-decker to assess the cost-effectiveness of converting front-engined buses for one-man-operation. Northern General was unhappy about the poor record of reliability of its early rear-engined buses which were not standing up to the rigorous OMO schedules. The Metro-Cammell Orion bodywork was originally of rear-entrance layout. A Routemaster-style bonnet was fitted and the rebuilt bus entered service as a 61-seater in 1972. This was the only PD3 to be so converted, although Northern General rebuilt a Routemaster in a similar style before abandoning such expensive conversions.

Ian Allan Library, Gavin Booth

Above:

This PD3 in the China Motor Bus fleet in Hong Kong is barely recognisable for what it is — an ex-Southdown vehicle converted to half-cab layout and fitted with a Birmingham-style bonnet. This conversion allows much better access to the engine than is possible with a full-width front. CMB purchased over 100 PD3s from Southdown.
M. Fowler

Below:

Alexander (Midland) converted some of its PD3/3s to quasi-PD3A specification as shown by the bus on the left which has been fitted with St Helens-style grille but retains the full-width bonnet top and therefore does not have the characteristic cut away of the PD3A at the front nearside corner.
SJB

Above:

Perhaps the most tasteless rebuilds were those operated as 'vintage buses' by Guards of London. This ex-Leicester PD3 has been fitted with a mock exposed radiator and has had its Metro-Cammell body rebuilt with an open staircase. Fun or vandalism? The choice is yours. *SJB*

Below:

The least obvious rebuilds were two Burlingham-bodied PD3/3s delivered to Scout Motor Services of Preston in 1958. These started out as PD2/20s but were converted to PD3 specification by Leyland before the chassis were delivered. They are not included in the table of PD3s on page 87. *A. Hustwitt*

Operational Experience – 20 years on

When the postwar PD-series Titan range was developed simplicity of design was still the keynote. Complexity came later, with the first generation of rear-engined double-deckers. With simplicity the buyer of a Titan automatically got reliability and the fact that a few PD3s have survived in service to the late-1980s bears witness to this. One of the operators still running PD3s is Green Bus Service of Great Wyrley, near Cannock, which operates three.

All three are in regular daily use and the proprietor of Green Bus Service, Mr Graham Martin is more than happy with their performance. 'At the end of the day I'm better off with a PD3', he says. 'Rear-engined buses are more costly and less reliable. For example they boil up in hot weather while a PD3 never overheats because its engine is where it should be.' In Mr Martin's experience rear-engined vehicles are more prone to fuel and oil leaks too, and suffer from excessive wear on the rear tyres — problems which he does not encounter on his Titans.

The Titans operated by Green Bus Service are a mixed bunch. The oldest is a PD3/3 with lowbridge Massey bodywork which was new in 1965 to Caerphilly UDC and came to Green Bus from Rhymney Valley UDC in April 1981 at a time when the company had an operational requirement for a lowbridge vehicle. This is the only rear-entrance PD3 in the fleet but it is fitted with platform doors.

'I wouldn't have an open-platform bus in service', says Mr Martin. 'It's not simply because of the draughts but more importantly because young children in this area are not used to buses without doors and I would be worried about the risk of accidents with children falling off. They're alright in London where children are brought up with them — but not here where they are an unfamiliar type.'

The former Rhymney Valley bus was Green Bus Service's first PD3 and it was followed in 1982 by the most modern, a 1969 PD3/14 which had been new to Stockport Corporation. This has a forward-entrance East Lancs body and, like the former Rhymney Valley vehicle, a manual gearbox and traditional exposed radiator. The last of the trio of PD3s joined the fleet in 1985 and came from Wilson of Carnwath but was new to Bradford Corporation. It dates from 1967 and has bodywork by East Lancs' erstwhile associate in Sheffield, Neepsend Coachworks. Like the former Stockport vehicle it is a forward entrance bus but unlike the other PD3s in the fleet it has a St Helens-style bonnet and a semi-automatic gearbox and is a PD3A/2.

How do they perform? In Mr Martin's words, 'They give remarkably little trouble'. They are used in all-day service and are allocated to routes which operate well away from the company's base — unlike the rear-engined vehicles which are generally allocated to routes passing close to the company's depot. The PD3s each average 3,000 miles a month; their slightly younger rear-engined stablemates each cover only 2,500 miles a month. The PD3s are not only more reliable but, predictably, they use less fuel. Their consumption averages around 10mpg compared with 7mpg on the company's Atlantean or 8mpg on a Gardner-engined Fleetline. Taken over a month's operation that extra fuel economy represents quite a significant saving. Interestingly there is no notable difference in the fuel consumption of the semi-automatic PD3.

Maintenance costs are low too with only one serious defect to record and that on the oldest of the trio. This needed a replacement engine — simply because of the age of the vehicle — and this was easily obtained from North's, the Yorkshire dealer, of whose spare parts service Mr Martin spoke very highly. 'They're very good; they've never supplied a bad engine'.

The former Stockport bus broke a layshaft which was repaired in-house while the one-time Bradford bus had a problem with gearbox vibration which the company was able to rectify. How many bus engineers wish they had as few faults to report on much more modern vehicles. . . .?

The drivers are happy with the PD3s despite the fact they lack power-assisted steering and that two of them have manual gearboxes — now an extremely rare feature on a double-deck bus.

And what of the future for these 20-year-old buses which are obsolete in the eyes of most bus operators? 'I have no plans to take them off the road. Why get rid of vehicles with proven reliability?' asks Mr Martin. I imagine that not a few engineers who lived through the traumatic times of the 1960s when front-engined buses were quite definitely out of favour and rear-engined buses were all the rage would agree with that sentiment.

A similar story of in-service reliability can be heard from another PD3 operator, Blackpool Borough Transport. Blackpool still runs a handful of PD3s which date from 1967-68 and each of which has covered some 650,000 miles. These have manual gearboxes and rear open-platform Metro-Cammell bodies. They are the only surviving British PD3s still in regular daily service with their original owner. Blackpool, like Green Bus Service, finds the Titans particularly fuel-efficient. Chief engineer Mr Bernard Browne, who recently retired, reported that they typically return figures of just over 9mpg. This is slightly lower than the Green Bus Service vehicles and reflects the different nature of Blackpool's urban operation which is perhaps more demanding than the largely interurban network of Green Bus Service. This figure is around 2mpg better than that of Blackpool's 33ft-long Atlanteans, although Mr Browne pointed out that the PD3s are both smaller and lighter. They weigh just over eight tons unladen, almost two tons lighter than most new double-deckers of the mid-1980s.

PD3 reliability in Blackpool is very good. They do not use many spares and those spares which are needed can easily be obtained. Indeed the most troublesome part of Blackpool's Titans has been the rear platform of the body which corrodes as a result of water being thrown up by the back wheels — but who will criticise body corrosion in a 20-year-old bus, particularly in the light of corrosion problems experienced in the 1980s by some fleets on vehicles less than three years old. But that, as they say, is another story. A seaside resort on the west coast — directly in the path of the prevailing winds — is going to be one of the worst places for corrosion with salt spray being blown in off the sea.

Blackpool Transport has no immediate plans to scrap its PD3s but in the new commercial environment of the deregulated bus business of the late 1980s they will clearly have to demonstrate that they can continue to be a cost-effective part of the fleet if they are to remain in service. This only time will tell.

Left:
Two of the three Green Bus PD3s in Cannock bus station in the summer of 1986. In the foreground is the bus which was new to Stockport Corporation; behind the one-time Bradford bus. *SJB*

Right:
The ex-Rhymney Valley PD3 is a lowbridge bus with rear entrance and platform doors. It was new in 1965 to Caerphilly and has Massey bodywork. *SJB*

Above:
The Bradford PD3 came via Wilson of Carnwath but spent much of its life with the West Yorkshire PTE. The Green Bus livery is two shades of green, yellow and cream — the yellow and cream being inspired by the ex-Rhymney Valley bus. *SJB*

Right:
Blackpool Transport is the last major operator of PD3s. *SJB*

Preserving the Species

The straightforward design of the PD3 Titan (and also of its short-wheelbase PD2 equivalent) has made the model an ideal candidate for enthusiasts interested in preservation. One pair of enthusiastic PD3 owners is Stuart Burton and Robert Smith who are restoring a former Stockport Corporation PD3/14 to original condition — and with a keen eye for detail.

The vehicle in question was Stockport Corporation 91. It was licensed on 1 January 1969, which makes it the last rear-platform bus to enter service in Britain. Its nearest rival, a Northampton Corporation Daimler, entered service in October 1968. The historic importance of this bus was one of the things which led to its preservation although the group formed to preserve it, of which Stuart and Robert are the sole survivors, had originally set their sights on an ex-Leigh Corporation lowbridge PD3A — which they missed by one day.

The group started saving to buy Stockport 91 (or Greater Manchester Transport 5891 as it was by then) 18 months before its withdrawal to avoid having to find large sums of money at short notice. The bus came out of service after the morning peak on 2 June 1982 and since then the painstaking work of restoration has been in progress.

The bus is kept at the Greater Manchester Transport Museum and this imposes certain disciplines on its owners. During the summer months, when the Museum is open to visitors, they have to share in the general tasks of running the Museum and even at the times when the Museum is closed there is a limit to the number of major jobs they can tackle since the premises have to be kept tidy. Thus the major work is done on the bus in the winter months when the Museum is not open to the public.

So far the PD3's simplicity has proved invaluable. No major mechanical problems have been encountered and none are antici-

pated. The front offside spring has been replaced and a new exhaust system fitted. Both of the vehicle's owners have had some engineering training but neither claim to be qualified mechanics. 'We learn as we go along — which is part of the fun', says Robert. The only area where they foresee some potentially difficult learning is in the braking system: the PD3/14 has air brakes, unlike most of the other vehicles in the Museum which are older and have vacuum brakes. Items like the electrical system are a major asset for restorers in that they have none of the complexity to be found on later types of buses. Another advantage of the PD3/14 is that it has a manual gearbox, eliminating the need for specialised knowledge or assistance which could have been required if it had been a Pneumocyclic model and any rectification work had been needed.

Although Stockport 91 is of an exceedingly conservative design, it is most certainly not a basic bus. Stockport's specification for the highbridge East Lancs body was a modern one, with no expense spared. The centre panel of the upper deck roof is of translucent glass fibre, giving a bright and airy appearance. The interior side lining panels are surfaced with plastic laminates, as are the seat backs. The seats themselves are covered in red leather. Fluorescent lighting and a strip bell-push are among the other modern features, underlining that despite its 1940s appearance this is quite definitely a bus of the late 1960s.

The body restoration has been undertaken with considerable thoroughness. The Selnec/Greater Manchester orange paint is difficult to paint over properly, so all the paint and transfers have been removed to eliminate any chance of them shining through when the body is repainted. Where necessary new aluminium panels have replaced damaged originals. Where non-original fixed windows were fitted on the upper deck they have been replaced by original pattern windows with opening top sections. Indicative of the attention to detail which Stuart and Robert are giving their bus, a non-original two-piece panel on the rear of the vehicle has been replaced by a single panel — an item that only the most eagle-eyed enthusiast would have noticed had it been left unchanged. Similarly the front dash panel, through which the mounting bolts for the windscreen washer reservoir protruded, has been replaced and the washer reservoir mounted on a concealed frame member. When undertaking repanelling work of this type the frame underneath has been rebuilt where necessary.

It is around the rear end that the biggest work has had to be undertaken. The rear platform is a weak spot on traditional double-deck bodies and on this vehicle the propensity for this area to rust has been exacerbated by the reaction of unpainted steel coming into contact with unpainted aluminium in the rear stress panel. This has been rectified, but it is a job which requires considerable care as the steel-framed body must be kept rigid while work is in progress.

Stockport Corporation 91 is one of 12 PD3s delivered towards the end of the undertaking's independent existence. Six of these had rear entrance bodies, while the other six introduced forward entrance double-deckers to the fleet. All 12 buses passed to the Selnec PTE on its formation and were repainted in Selnec orange and white. And although this batch of PD3s is generally associated with services in the Stockport area, where 91 was running when finally withdrawn, this bus did spend some of its life with Selnec at Oldham. When Stuart and Robert have finished on No 91 it will be repainted in Stockport's red and white livery with black lining-out, complete with transfers of the town's municipal crest.

Their choice of a PD3 was not influenced solely by the historic significance of Stockport 91 as the last of a long line of open platform buses in Britain, nor by its simplicity although this was clearly important. Other factors came into play. Stuart points out that it is representative of many municipal buses in the northwest, where both Leyland and East Lancs had regular buyers for their products. And there is also the question of personal involvement. Both of 91's owners remember seeing Stockport's PD3s in service and say that this is important to them. They can relate to this vehicle in a way which they cannot relate to earlier generations of buses.

The restoration of any vehicle of this size is a slow process and Stuart stresses that they each only work on the bus when they want to (which is still quite a lot of the time!). Bus preservation is a hobby and the work has to be pleasurable — and if a job is undertaken under pressure then there is more likelihood of it not being done properly.

The proof of Stuart Burton's and Robert Smith's enthusiasm and of the pleasure they have obtained in restoring Stockport 91 will surely be evident from the high standards of the bus when it is finished. And when will that be? True to their philosophy of working on the bus for pleasure neither will say. But whenever it is, the result will be a PD3 worth seeing.

Right:
Stockport 91 when new. This is the condition to which it is being restored.
S. Burton collection

Above:
The bus spent most of its working life in orange and white — here it has Selnec Southern fleetnames while operating in Oldham.
S. Burton collection

Below:
When withdrawn it had returned to Stockport and carried Greater Manchester fleetnames. The rearmost opening windows on the upper deck — visible in the previous picture — had by this time been removed. They have been reinstated as part of the body restoration. *S. Burton collection*

PD3:
Customers in the British Isles

Operator	Quantity
AA Motor Services, Ayr	1
Accrington Corporation	9
W. Alexander & Sons, Falkirk	102 a
Ayrshire Bus Owners (A1 Service), Ardrossan	1
Bedwas & Machen UDC	1
Baxter, Hanley	1 b
Blackpool Corporation	90
Bolton Corporation	43
Bournemouth Corporation	30
Bradford Corporation	30
Brighton Corporation	5
Burnley, Colne & Nelson JTC	6
Bury Corporation	25
Caerphilly UDC	8
Cardiff Corporation	6
Carmichael (Highland), Glenboig	1
Central SMT	10
Chieftain (Laurie), Hamilton	2
Clark & Rose, Aberdeen	3 c
Coras Iompair Eireann	152 d
County Motors, Lepton	2
Darwen Corporation	5
Delaine, Bourne	2
Doncaster Corporation	10
East Midland Motor Services	12
Edinburgh Corporation	81
Gateshead & District	5
Glasgow Corporation	140
Halifax	16
Harper Bros, Heath Hayes	3
Haslingden Corporation	2
Huddersfield Corporation	24
Hudson, Horncastle	1
Isle of Man Road Services	6
James, Ammanford	2
Lancashire United Transport	14
Leeds City Transport	91
Leicester City Transport	117
Leigh Corporation	2
Lloyd, Bagilt	1
Llynfi Motor Services, Maesteg	1
London Transport	9 c
Merthyr Tydfil Corporation	33
Newcastle Corporation	10
Northern General Transport	20
OK Motor Services, Bishop Auckland	1
Oldham Corporation	10

Operator	Quantity
PMT	16
Portsmouth Corporation	5
Preston Corporation	26
Ramsbottom UDC	8 e
Rawtenstall Corporation	12
Ribble Motor Services	236
Scout, Preston	3
Severn, Stainforth	6
Sheffield Corporation	30
Skill, Nottingham	2
Southdown Motor Services	285
Southend Corporation	21
South Notts, Gotham	34
South Yorkshire, Pontefract	2
Stockport Corporation	27
Stratford Blue	15
Sunderland District	13
Trent Motor Traction	22
Turner, Brown Edge	2
Tynemouth	12
Tyneside	3
Ulster Transport Authority	142
Wallace Arnold, Leeds	7
Weardale Motor Services, Frosterley	1
Western SMT	186
Wigan Corporation	36
Yorkshire Traction	45
Yorkshire Woollen	9
Total	2,352

Notes

a The last 25 vehicles ordered by Alexander were delivered in 1961 to the newly formed Alexander (Midland) and Alexander (Northern) companies. The former received 18, the latter seven.

b Delivered direct to PMT which took over the Baxter business.

c Non-PSV.

d Delivered as completely knocked down (CKD) kits for assembly by CIE.

e The last Ramsbottom vehicle was delivered to the Selnec PTE which had taken over the Ramsbottom operation.

Exports: In addition 816 PD3s were exported, all but two as CKD kits. The biggest single customer was Ashok Leyland, which took 378 for sale to customers in India. Exports accounted for 26% of total PD3 production.

The Lowlander

Operators who needed high-capacity buses to run in areas with low bridges had, since the launch of the original Titan in 1927, generally opted for lowbridge bodywork with an offside sunken gangway. This layout created two difficulties. On the upper deck the bench seats for four passengers made it difficult for passengers to get in and out of their seats: on the lower deck the sunken gangway was liable to be struck by the heads of passengers getting out of their seats on the offside. First Bristol, then AEC, and finally Dennis (under licence from Bristol) all tackled this problem in the early 1950s with special lowheight designs — the Lodekka, Bridgemaster and Loline respectively — which featured low chassis frames and complex rear axle designs to allow a conventional centre gangway on both decks within an overall height of around 13ft 6in.

Leyland's first sortie into the lowheight bus business produced the unconventional rear-engined Low-Loader prototypes which ultimately diverted the company's intention away from the aim of low overall height to a new concept of high-capacity rear-engined buses and to the successful Atlantean. However, under pressure from the Scottish Bus Group, which in the late 1950s was buying around 100 Titans a year with lowbridge bodywork, Leyland's engineers reconsidered the need for a lowheight bus and came up with what was in effect a lowheight PD3: the Lowlander.

In common with the PD3 this had an 18ft 6in wheelbase, a Leyland O.600 engine (but rated at 140bhp) and a choice of synchromesh or Pneumocyclic gearboxes. It used the glass fibre bonnet and grille of the PD3A. But where it differed from the PD3 was in its low wide frame and its rear axle. The frame dropped down behind the front axle and was wide enough to accommodate the remote-mounted gearbox under the nearside seats in mid-wheelbase without the gearbox intruding into the gangway. The rear axle was a new double-reduction drop-centre unit with the differential offset to the nearside. (This later found use, turned to face the rear, in the lowheight PDR1/2 Atlantean.)

Four models were offered, all with air brakes:

Model	Gearbox
LR1	Pneumocyclic
LR3	Synchromesh
LR5	Pneumocyclic, rear air suspension
LR7	Synchromesh, rear air suspension

No LR5 models were built.

The Lowlander was built at Leyland's Scottish plant — Albion Motors — in Glasgow and was sold as an Albion in Scotland and as a Leyland in England. Two sales brochures, identical but for the Albion name on one and the Leyland name on the other, were produced to support the Lowlander's launch at the 1961 Scottish Motor Show. The Scottish Bus Group immediately ordered 106 for 1962 delivery, of which fewer than 20 were delivered and in service by the end of the year — by which time repeat orders had been placed for 1963, on the assumption that with the use of well-proven Titan components the Lowlander would provide Titan reliability. It did not. The Lowlanders proved troublesome and many of those bought for use on intensive urban services in the industrial belt of central Scotland were quickly reallocated to lighter work in the Highlands.

Comparatively few Lowlanders were sold in England and none was exported. Out of a total production of 274, 194 were bought by SBG companies. Lowlander production ceased in 1966.

John Aldridge adds . . .

The poor sales of the Lowlander were no doubt a disappointment — and a surprise — to Leyland. They may well have resulted in part from efforts by Leyland engineers (or the cost accountants) to keep the number of special

An LR3 chassis drawing. *Leyland*

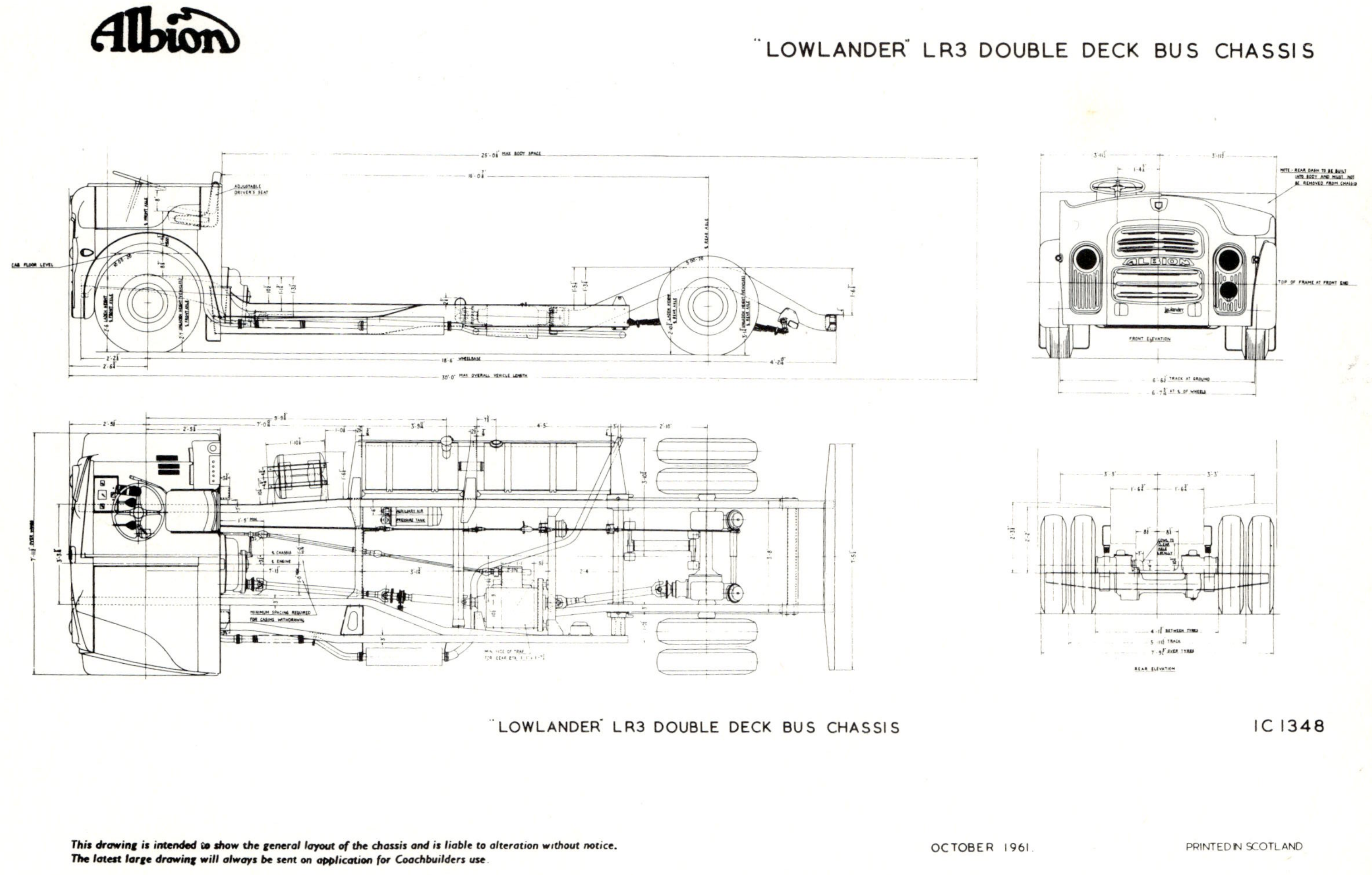

Albion
"LOWLANDER" LR3 DOUBLE DECK BUS CHASSIS
FRONT ELEVATION
REAR ELEVATION
"LOWLANDER" LR3 DOUBLE DECK BUS CHASSIS
IC 1348
This drawing is intended to show the general layout of the chassis and is liable to alteration without notice.
The latest large drawing will always be sent on application for Coachbuilders use.
OCTOBER 1961.
PRINTED IN SCOTLAND

parts to a minimum. Thus the Lowlander used a standard PD3 front end assembly, which meant that the cab roof intruded into the front of the upper deck saloon. That did not ease matters for the bodybuilder, and also gave low headroom for the passengers at the front of the upper deck.

It was rumoured that Leyland was unwilling to develop the Lowlander, and only did so at the insistence of the Scottish Bus Group (SBG). It was said to have offered a special additional discount of £150 per chassis if SBG took lowheight Atlanteans instead, but SBG declined. Later, SBG added insult to injury, in a manner of speaking, by not ordering more Lowlanders but turning to the then opposition and buying Daimler Fleetlines.

One or two other features on the Lowlander were also not to the liking of some operators, for example the remotely mounted gearbox. That might be essential in such a lowfloor design, but it did mean that changing a gearbox was a more difficult operation than usual, unless the operator had a cutaway pit.

The total production of 274 Lowlanders was probably below even the most pessimistic view of sales prospects, which is no doubt why it left Leyland with a considerable surplus of spare parts on its hands: for example brand-new chassis side members, many of which were eventually sold for scrap.

But it must not be thought that the Lowlander was a dated or cheap design. For example, the first batch of 10 bought by Ribble were the first buses in its fleet with a dual line air braking system, in which front and rear brakes are on separate circuits, so that a failure in one still leaves the other fully operational. The 10 were also the first in the Ribble fleet to have air assisted handbrakes.

Specification

1962 model Albion Lowlander

Engine	Leyland O.600 9.8 litre (597cu in) six-cylinder diesel rated at 140bhp at 1,700rpm
Gearbox	a) Remote-mounted Leyland four-speed synchromesh with direct-drive top coupled to a 16¼in diameter clutch b) Remote-mounted Leyland four-speed semi-automatic Pneumocyclic with direct-drive top coupled to an 18in diameter fluid coupling with lock-up clutch
Rear axle	Stepped double-reduction with offset spiral bevel with a choice of four ratios: 5.41, 5.87, 6.40 or 7.00 to 1
Suspension	Conventional 4in wide semi-elliptic leaf springs, 4ft 2in long on the front axle, 5ft 2in long on the rear
Brakes	Front 5in wide, rear 8in wide with total lining area of 702sq in. Air operated
Fuel tank	Twin interconnected tanks of 38gal capacity
Tyres	10.00 × 20 front, twin 9.00 × 20 rear
Electrics	24V (CAV) with 55A dc dynamo and 174A/hr CAV, Exide or Oldham battery. AC equipment also available
Instruments	Electric speedometer with mileage recorder; oil pressure gauge; oil pressure warning light; dual air pressure gauge; water temperature gauge; steering-column-mounted horn and dip switch
Steering	Manual Marles cam-and-double-roller with 22in diameter steering wheel requiring 4¾ turns from lock to lock
Chassis weight	5tons 8cwt 2qrs

Below:
The wide entrance and low flat floor of an Alexander-bodied Lowlander. *SJB collection*

Photofeature:
An A to Y of Lowlanders

This section, like that on PD3s before it, illustrates every operator which bought a new Lowlander, from Alexander (Fife) to Yorkshire Woollen. A list — a very short list — of Lowlander customers appears on page 76. Chassis numbers are listed in Appendix 2.

Below:
In 1963 the demonstrator, originally painted in Glasgow Corporation yellow and green, was repainted maroon and white and went into service with Edinburgh Corporation. Neither Edinburgh nor Glasgow needed lowheight double-deckers and neither bought Lowlanders. One ordered by Edinburgh was eventually sold to Western SMT.
SJB

Above and below:
The demonstrator was bought by Bamber Bridge Motor Services and is seen here in Bamber Bridge in 1966. It passed to Ribble when Bamber Bridge was taken over in 1967, and had a later style of front dome fitted to allow a two-line destination display. *G. R. Mills, R. Marshall*

Top right:
Alexander (Fife) was created in 1961 and inherited a double-deck fleet with a strong bias towards Gardner engines — all of the most modern 'deckers were Bristol Lodekkas. So an order for seven of Albion's new Lowlander was unexpected.

These LR1s were the first buses in the fleet with fluid transmission and were Fife's only new Lowlanders although a number of secondhand examples were added to the fleet. Alexander built the bodywork. *R. Marshall*

Right:
Alexander (Midland) had a big fleet of lowbridge PD3s and the lowheight Lowlander was a natural progression. In two years 44 were purchased, all with Alexander bodywork. Note the Lowlander badge above the right hand end of the numberplate and the Albion badge on the radiator filler flap. *SJB*

ALBION
7417 SP

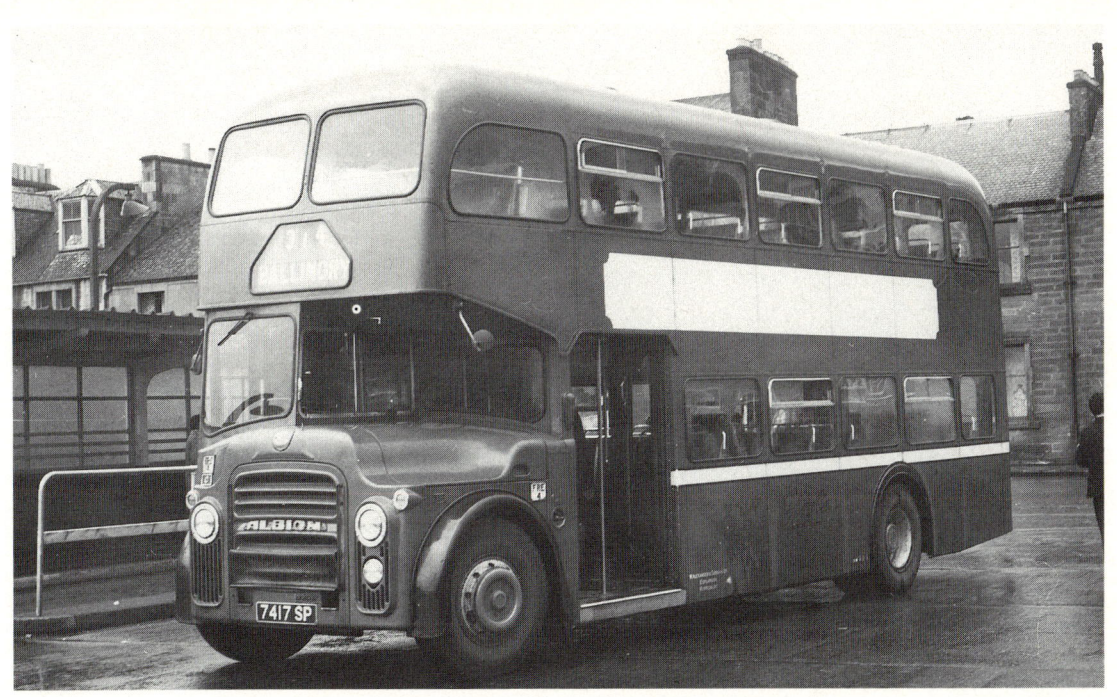

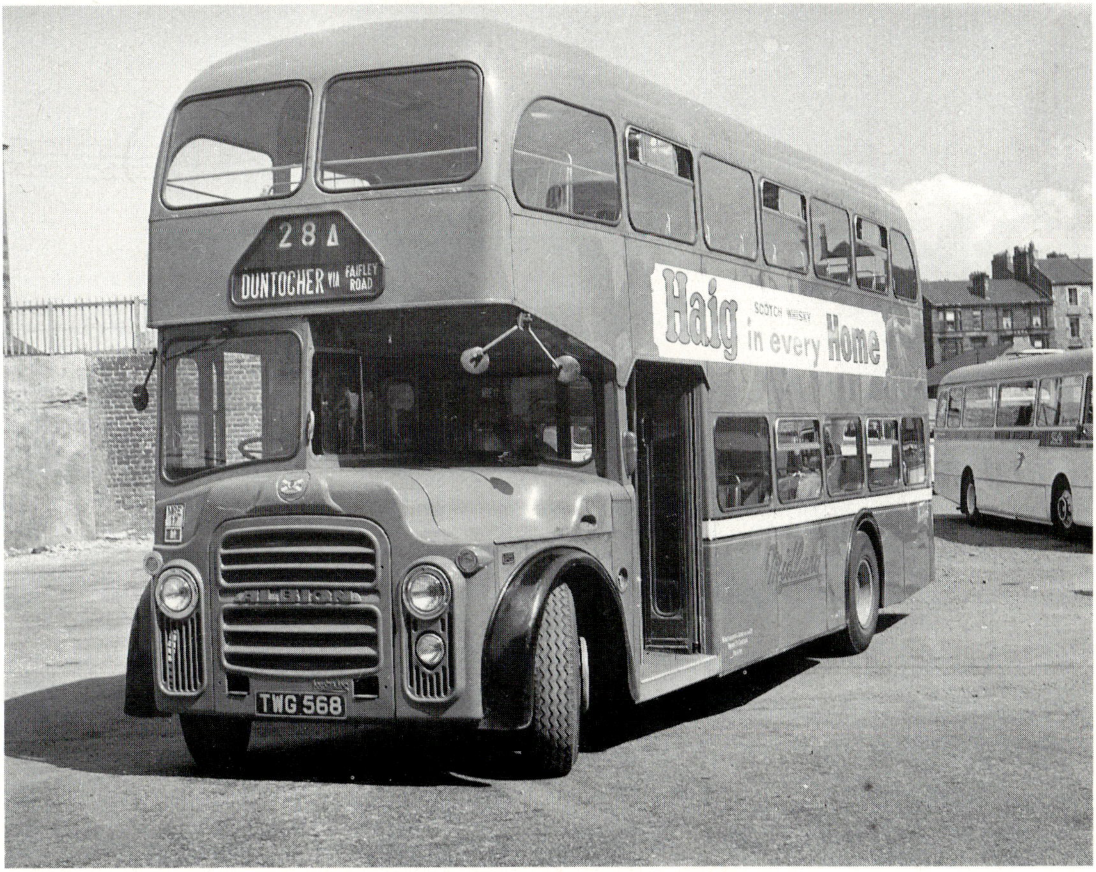
28A
DUNTOCHER VIA FAIFLEY ROAD
Haig SCOTCH WHISKY in every Home
TWG 568

Above:
Alexander (Northern), like Midland, was a PD3 user. Two Lowlanders were delivered in 1961 and were to be its last new double-deckers for over 15 years. For most Scottish Bus Group companies the Lowlanders were the last Leyland-engined double-deckers to be purchased. *SJB*

Centre left:
Central SMT bought 30 Lowlanders. The first, with Northern Counties 71-seat bodywork, was exhibited at the 1962 Commercial Motor Show. Northern Counties managed to disguise the Lowlander's high driving position rather more successfuly than did Alexander. Northern Counties bodied 20 Central Lowlanders. *SJB*

Left:
The other 10 Central Lowlanders had Alexander bodies. The Lowlanders were at the time the only semi-automatic buses ever ordered by Central. This one is seen in East Kilbride in 1963. In 1965 all of Central's Lowlanders were banished to less arduous operations with Alexander (Fife) and Highland Omnibuses. *SJB*

Right:
The biggest English user of the Lowlander — with 18 — was East Midland Motor Services. The first 14 had Alexander 72-seat bodies and were new in 1963. Note the Leyland lettering on the grille which was a feature of English Lowlanders. This vehicle was photographed in Doncaster bus station in April 1963. All of the East Midland vehicles were LR7s with manual gearboxes and rear air suspension. A Yorkshire Traction PD3A is visible behind. *M. Fowler*

Left:
The last four East Midland Lowlanders were the only examples to be bodied by Metro-Cammell, although they were to the same design as some earlier vehicles built by Weymann for Yorkshire Woollen. The shallow windows disguised the low overall height of the body and the high driving position. This example is seen in 1974 in NBC green livery. It was new in 1966. *G. R. Mills*

Below left:
Luton Corporation had a fleet of lowbridge PD2s and had then tried the Dennis Loline. When the Lowlander was announced it was seen as a logical successor to the PD2 and 16 were ordered. They were delivered in 1963 and had 65-seat bodywork by East Lancs (10) and Neepsend (six) which had a short rear overhang on a standard 18ft 6in wheelbase chassis. The Luton Lowlanders were LR7s. This was Luton's last, with Neepsend body.
A. J. Douglas

Left:

Ribble had lowbridge PD2s and lowbridge Atlanteans. All of its PD3s were highbridge buses and so the Lowlander was an obvious choice for use on routes needing lowheight vehicles. Alexander, with their experience in bodying the model, were given the body order for a batch of 10 in 1963 followed by a further six in 1965. Full fronts were fitted to give the Lowlanders some family resemblance to the PD3s but the end result was not really aesthetically pleasing. Ribble's Lowlanders were LR1s with Pneumocyclic gearboxes. Blackburn bus station in 1967 is the location of this view. *R. L. Wilson*

Left:

South Notts bought five Lowlanders with Northern Counties bodywork. They were the only Northern Counties-bodied Lowlanders sold in England, and South Notts was the only independent to buy new Lowlanders. As well as having Leyland grilles they had South Notts name plates affixed below the radiator filler as shown on this 1964 vehicle photographed in Nottingham in 1981. The South Notts buses were the only LR3s built. *A. R. Kaye*

Right:

Southend Corporation, like most Lowlander customers, had previously bought lowbridge PD3s. Ten Lowlanders were purchased and had Alexander bodies with a comprehensive destination display squeezed into the limited space available. They were new in 1963 and this one is seen at Shoeburyness in April of that year. They were later equipped for one-man operation.
G. R. Mills

Above:
The first Lowlander chassis was bodied by Alexander for Western SMT and was an exhibit at the 1961 Scottish Motor Show. It entered service in 1962 but only ran for Western for four years before being transferred to Highland Omnibuses. It was an LR1. *SJB*

Below:
Western bought 111 Lowlanders, making them by far the biggest user of the type. Most had Alexander bodywork. *SJB*

Lowlander Customers

Operator	Quantity
Albion demonstrator	1
W. Alexander & Sons (Fife)	7
W. Alexander & Sons (Midland)	44
W. Alexander & Sons (Northern)	2
Central SMT	30
East Midland Motor Services	18
Luton Corporation	16
Ribble Motor Services	16
Southend Corporation	10
South Notts, Gotham	5
Western SMT	111a
Yorkshire Woollen	14
Total	274

Note
a Including one chassis built for Edinburgh Corporation but not used by them.

Below:
Only three British Electric Traction group companies bought Lowlanders — East Midland, Ribble and Yorkshire Woollen. There were 14 for Yorkshire Woollen and these had 72-seat Weymann bodies on LR7 chassis. This one was photographed in 1975. *A. J. Douglas*

Points of Detail

Above and left:
The original concealed radiator for the PD3 was that used on the PD2 but, except on the first two chassis, with the addition of an extra cooling grille at the bottom. There was a choice of torpedo-type sidelights mounted alongside the headlamps (above) or of integral sidelights mounted higher on the bonnet (left). The integral lights are shown on a Glasgow Corporation vehicle with non-standard Leyland Albion Titan badging. *Roe, Alexander*

Above and below:
The PD3A, too, came with a choice of sidelight types. The extra spotlight on the Wallace Arnold **vehicle reflects Yorkshire's weather. Lowlanders generally had integral sidelights, although there were a few exceptions.** *Ian Allan Library, G. R. Mills*

Right:
The first Lowlanders had torpedo sidelights. Those sold in Scotland had Albion lettering and an Albion badge on the radiator filler flap. English vehicles had standard PD3A fronts but with the addition of the Lowlander name above the numberplate, a feature of all Lowlanders.
Albion

Below:
Leyland Diesel lettering was applied to the bonnet side on exposed radiator and concealed radiator PD3s. On PD3As there was a small badge on the radiator filler cap. *SJB*

Bottom:
Lowlander and PD3A grilles were interchangeable, as illustrated by this Albion Titan PD3A in the Alexander (Midland) fleet. *SJB*

Roadtest

Quick off the mark, but hard on the ears

Gavin Booth

I had been a surrogate PD3 driver since 1964, when Edinburgh Corporation put the first of a batch of 50 PD3s on my local route, and as a top deck passenger I would mentally change gear and brake in unison with the driver sitting below. This helped prepare me for Western Scottish 1685 — although not for the heavy steering.

We had chosen a route from 1685's home base at Kilmarnock, in fact one of the most famous bus routes in central Scotland: the corridor to Ardrossan. This 15-mile route links the two towns, passing through the new town of Irvine and several smaller communities on the way. It is served throughout by Western and independent co-operative A1 Service, and between Irvine and Ardrossan by a second co-operative, AA Motor Services.

The route undulates gently with no severe inclines, but with a growing number of roundabouts and mini roundabouts to test the steering. The centre of Kilmarnock, in spite of a complex one-way system, can be congested, but there are useful stretches of open road to make up time.

The driving cab of 1685 was typical of Leylands of the period, although the famous square speedometer had been replaced by a tachograph; the only other instrument was the vacuum gauge. The flasher controls were rather awkwardly positioned on a branch from the steering column, with the horn push at the end.

Visibility was good, helped by the scalloped bonnet corner of the St Helens-style front, and by the high-set driving position. Many drivers would agree that this vantage point, a consequence of the front-set axle and forward control layout, has rarely been bettered on subsequent breeds of bus. Early rear-engined buses ran into the problem of low driving positions, and some operators artificially raised the position in answer to staff complaints.

Certainly, the view from 1685 was excellent with a deep screen, ample cab side windows and good mirrors. The sliding driver's door, unusual on a Scottish bus, was appreciated, as it allowed greater permutations of heating and ventilating.

We started off from Western's Nursery Avenue headquarters, and launched into Kilmarnock's one-way system, joining the route to Ardrossan. The first part of the route, through suburban Kilmarnock, carries much of the westbound traffic from the town, and can be fairly congested. A bypass eventually takes through traffic heading towards Irvine, Ardrossan and the north, but the bus route sticks to the old road, with conveniently spaced communities like Crosshouse and Dreghorn to top up the passenger loads, as well as bigger centres like Irvine, Kilwinning and Saltcoats.

Performance was good, but the bus was virtually unladen, so the engine was not worked too hard. Rear and underfloor engines spoil a driver for engine noise, so the roar of the O.600 came as a slight shock, particularly with the exhaust note reverberating off high walls.

Having been trained on the Bristol FLFs normally used by SBG fleets, with their notoriously unforgiving crash gearboxes, the synchromesh box on 1685 caused me no problems. By the time the bus was built in 1961, Leyland had reverted to a gearbox that only had synchromesh on third and fourth gears, but it was rarely necessary to change down below third. Starting off in second gear was no problem, although with a full load of 75 passengers this could cause differential wear — and often did. In a loaded PD3 there was always the feeling that the mechanical specification was not quite up to it; the model was, after all, basically an extended PD2.

Early Atlanteans with the 9.8-litre O.600 engine suffered in the same way. The engine had been developed at a time when double-deck buses had 56 seats and weighed around 7.5 tons. Now double-deckers were longer and heavier, and the power unit was asked to propel up to 78 passengers plus standees. The 11.1-litre O.680 engine was the answer, a development of the O.600, and this helped transform performance on later Atlanteans, though PD3s soldiered on with the older unit.

Vacuum brakes were not really the flavour of the month by 1961, but they allowed smooth, progressive braking on 1685. It was the low-geared steering that was surprisingly heavy, needing a fair effort to negotiate hazards on the route. Just a few weeks earlier I had driven one of Clydeside's Routemasters, a bus of roughly similar vintage, but with power-assisted steering, hydraulic brakes and automatic transmission, which can tend to colour your judgement, but given SBG's requirement for basic-specification buses, the horses-for-courses rule probably applied.

SBG's ability to buy Bristol/ECW products *and* proprietary makes meant that three of its fleets bought side-by-side batches of Lodekkas and Titans. These usually went to different depots, and so they were not indiscriminately mixed, but their utilisation did not always seem to match the characteristics of the vehicle. Thus one could find a Leyland Titan, to many people essentially an urban bus, on some of SBG's classic long-haul, inter-urban routes, and Lodekkas, buses that traditionally took a lot of 'winding up', on urban services with tight frequencies.

SBG companies bought almost 300 synchromesh-gearbox PD3s between 1957 and 1961, all with vacuum brakes. The simple specification was favoured by the Group, which chose not to buy the alternative Pneumocyclic-gearbox PD3s; when SBG changed to the lowheight Albion Lowlander in 1962, Leyland actually dropped the PD3A/3 variant.

Compared with the more ponderous Bristol FLF, the engine and gearbox combination on the Western PD3 allowed for quick acceleration, and we had little difficulty keeping up with the A1 Fleetlines on the road to Ardrossan.

The PD3 was well suited to the stop-start Kilmarnock-Ardrossan route, and while there is a certain personal satisfaction achieving clean gearchanges on a crash-box FLF, the easy synchromesh on the PD3 eased the driver's burden, and permitted full concentration to be devoted to safe driving.

At full speed, though — an indicated 45mph — the noise in the driver's cab was probably more than most modern drivers would regularly tolerate. We had 1685 for an afternoon, so the noise problem was not too great; perhaps after an 8hr shift, I might have been less charitable. Otherwise, it was difficult to fault 1685. Leyland's long experience of building Titans, going back over 30 years, was reflected in the efficient, rugged simplicity of this bus, which performed well, and made the driver's job relatively easy, except for the steering.

Left:
The test PD3 spent most of its life allocated to Western SMT's Ardrossan depot. Here it passes the level crossing in Ardrossan; its now-closed home depot was just off the picture to the right. *SJB*

Above:
The 30ft long lowbridge Alexander body looked sleek when it was new. Now it looks small when compared with 1980s buses with squared profiles and deep windows. The fuel economy message on the side is particularly appropriate on a high-capacity lightweight bus such as this. *SJB*

Below:
The interior is functional rather than stylish. The sunken gangway provides almost 6ft of headroom but the bench seats can be difficult to get in and out of on a crowded bus, particularly for passengers sitting at the nearside who have to squeeze past three other people to reach the gangway. *SJB*

Above:
Ardrossan has changed little since the PD3 was delivered. This is Glasgow Street and only the cars in the background tell that this picture was taken in 1986, not 1966. *SJB*

Below:
There is plenty of space to get at the engine when you lean over the nearside wing. Items needing routine checks are easily accessible. *SJB*

The Passengers' Viewpoint

Loud noise and quietness are paradoxically the overriding impressions of a trip in an empty PD3. On tickover there is no noise at all — nor is there any vibration. When the bus is standing still it is as if the engine has cut out; indeed, I thought it had stalled at the first junction at which we stopped. But when moving it is extremely noisy, in the lower saloon at any rate. Conversation with Western Scottish Inspector Harry Hay, who accompanied us on the test, involved a lot of shouting, even on the rear platform, to overcome noise from the transmission — some of which Harry Hay suspected was coming from the centre bearing on the propeller shaft. He recollected that PD2s were generally quieter than PD3s and attributed this to the one-piece propshaft on the shorter model. In the upper saloon things were much quieter, with conversation being carried out in normal tones.

The ride varied. At the extreme rear it was very lively, no doubt partly because the vehicle was unladen. At the front of the upper deck it was lively too — the front seats are almost directly over the front axle. But in mid-wheelbase the ride was firm without being harsh and one is forced to ask if passengers really do notice the difference in ride offered by modern air-suspended buses.

The Alexander body on the test PD3 was typical of many supplied to Scottish Bus Group operators with 67 seats (35 up, 32 down). It was of side gangway lowbridge layout and like most bodies of the time had a fairly simple standard of interior finish with red-painted interior side panels (matching the red leather-cloth seats), conventional tungsten lighting (fluorescent tubes first appeared in SBG buses just a couple of years later) and single-skin glass fibre domes. Heating was provided by one underseat blower at the front of the upper deck and an outlet on the lower deck front bulkhead. Heavy manually-operated platform doors at the rear helped to keep the heat in — Scottish bus conductresses must have been a muscular breed.

Clearly it is unfair to compare a 25-year-old bus with its 1980s counterparts yet in most comparisons the PD3 would hold up well. It was warm, comfortable and fairly smooth, with only the high noise level in the lower deck militating against it. The body was firm and rattle-free. I would have been happy to make a local journey on it — indeed the citizens of Kilmarnock still do on occasion. The PD3 is licensed as a PSV and can be pressed into service if required.

When they were new, Western's PD3s tended to be used on long-distance interurban services such as those from Glasgow to Greenock, Ayr and even Stranraer; the last-named would be a bit of a marathon now — yet not an impossible one if one were comfortably tucked away from the noise at the front of the upper deck. Even today, the PD3 remains a perfectly acceptable bus for the passenger.

Postscript –
The Ashok Leyland Titan

The front-engined Titan still lives. Almost 20 years after the last PD3 rolled off the assembly line in Lancashire, the biggest single export customer, Ashok Leyland in India, is still making a PD3-based double-decker; the ALPD Titan.

The ALPD is manufactured at Ashok Leyland's Madras plant and features a choice of engines — the 6.54-litre AL402, a development of the O.400 best known in Britain in late-model Tiger Cubs, or the 11.1-litre AL680, a locally-manufactured version of the O.680. The ALPD has an 18ft 6in wheelbase, air brakes, leaf springs, and a gross vehicle weight of 16 tons. A four-speed synchromesh gearbox is standard, although an Indian-built Pneumo-cyclic can also be fitted.

Below:
Ashok Leyland still build what is basically a PD3, as illustrated by this gargantuan specimen operating in Bombay in 1983. It is one of some 800 operated by the Bombay Electricity Supply and Transport undertaking. *SJB*

Current production is around 170 chassis a year and Ashok Leyland Titans can be seen in service in most Indian cities.

Specification

1984 model Ashok Leyland Titan ALPD

Engine	Ashok Leyland AL402 6.54 litre (400cu in) six-cylinder diesel rated at 135bhp at 2,400rpm. The Ashok Leyland AL680 is available as an option
Gearbox	Ashok Leyland four-speed synchromesh with direct-drive top coupled to a 14in diameter clutch
Rear axle	Single reduction spiral bevel with a ratio of 6.14 to 1
Suspension	Conventional semi-elliptic leaf springs
Brakes	Air operated
Fuel tank	36gal capacity
Tyres	11.00 × 20 front, twin 10.00 × 20 rear
Electrics	24V with 30A alternator and 135A/hr battery
Steering	Recirculating ball with 21in diameter steering wheel

Left and below:
Ashok Leyland has supplied only one Titan to an operator outside India. When Hong Kong's bus operators were complaining about the unreliability of rear-engined buses this ALPD1 was supplied to the China Motor Bus Company. When new it had a full-width cab; it was later rebuilt with a conventional half-cab and a Birmingham-style bonnet. It had bodywork built in India by Sion.
Ian Allan Library, M. Fowler

Appendix 1:
Leyland Titan PD3 Chassis List

The following list contains all PD3 chassis in numerical order and gives a broad illustration of the operators whose chassis were being built at any given time. All of the export chassis (which includes those for CIE) were manufactured as CKD kits and shipped in boxes for assembly at their destination with the exception of 802657, the Indonesian PD3/11, and 700338 for Ashok Leyland which were shipped as fully assembled chassis.

When PD3 production commenced the Leyland chassis numbering system used the first two numbers to indicate the year of manufacture — thus 560283 was the 283rd chassis of 1956. This system continued until 1962, when it was replaced by a new series starting with the letter L and followed by five numbers. This system was in turn replaced by a new system in which the first digit of a six figure number showed the year of manufacture. In 1970 there came a reversion to the earlier type of year identification, this time using the first two digits of a seven figure number. Thus 703743 was a 1967 chassis for Stockport while 7003746 was a 1970 chassis for Ashok Leyland.

Chassis No	Model	Customer
560283	PD3/2	Potteries
570002	PD3/1	Laurie (Chieftan), Hamilton
570208	PD3/4	East Midland
570409-410	PD3/4	East Midland
570556	PD3/4	Ribble
570704-705	PD3/4	Ribble
570706-707	PD3/4	East Midland
570742	PD3/4	Ribble
570743-744	PD3/4	East Midland
570831-834	PD3/4	Ribble
570859-860	PD3/4	Ribble
570873-874	PD3/4	James, Ammanford
570875-876	PD3/4	Potteries
570906-908	PD3/4	Potteries
571004-005	PD3/4	Ribble
571017-020	PD3/4	Potteries
571183-184	PD3/4	Potteries
571208-211	PD3/4	Potteries
571290-294	PD3/4	Ribble
571300-301	PD3/4	Ribble
571380	PD3/2	Edinburgh
571497-500	PD3/4	Ribble
571501-502	PD3/1	Newcastle
571555-559	PD3/4	Ribble
571578-583	PD3/1	Newcastle
571590-591	PD3/1	Newcastle
571650-654	PD3/4	Ribble
571729-734	PD3/4	Ribble
571756-760	PD3/4	Southdown
571774-778	PD3/4	Southdown
571786	PD3/4	Llynfi, Maesteg
571818-822	PD3/4	Southdown

Chassis No	Model	Customer
571859-865	PD3/3	Western SMT
571873-877	PD3/3	Western SMT
571897-901	PD3/3	Western SMT
571906-910	PD3/3	Central SMT
571924-928	PD3/3	Central SMT
572291	PD3/3	Hudson, Horncastle
572313	PD3/1	Export (Finlay)
572314-318	PD3/4	Ribble
572321-324	PD3/4	Ribble
572335-338	PD3/4	Ribble
572356-359	PD3/4	Trent
572471-475	PD3/3	Alexander
572501-506	PD3/4	Ribble
572563-567	PD3/4	Ribble
572574-579	PD3/4	Ribble
572593-594	PD3/3	Alexander
572619-621	PD3/3	Alexander
572660-664	PD3/4	Trent
572675-679	PD3/4	Trent
572770-774	PD3/4	Trent
572844	PD3/2	Laurie (Chieftan), Hamilton
572845-847	PD3/4	Trent
573019	PD3/2	Edinburgh
573065-068	PD3/4	Ribble
573089-093	PD3/4	East Midland
573187	PD3/5	Severn, Stainforth
573304-308	PD3/4	Ribble
573332-334	PD3/4	Ribble
573374-379	PD3/4	Ribble
573467-470	PD3/3	Alexander
573511-514	PD3/3	Alexander
573525-527	PD3/3	Alexander

Chassis No	Model	Customer	Chassis No	Model	Customer
573539-544	PD3/4	Ribble	581291-295	PD3/4	Merthyr Tydfil
573588	PD3/3	Alexander	581300-303	PD3/3	Western SMT
573607-610	PD3/4	Ribble	581472-474	PD3/3	Alexander
573632-633	PD3/4	Ribble	581490-493	PD3/3	Alexander
573654-655	PD3/4	Ribble	581503	PD3/3	Alexander
573668	PD3/5	Bolton	581662-663	PD3/3	Alexander
573715	PD3/5	Bolton	581703-704	PD3/3	Alexander
573855	PD3/5	Bolton	581724-728	PD3/4	Lancashire United
573864-865	PD3/5	Bolton	581754-757	PD3/2	CIE
573871	PD3/5	Bolton	581758-761	PD3/4	Lancashire United
573874-875	PD3/5	Bolton	581774-776	PD3/4	Lancashire United
573920-921	PD3/5	Bolton	581818-819	PD3/4	Lancashire United
573930-931	PD3/4	Ribble	581894-896	PD3/3	Alexander
573952-953	PD3/4	Ribble	581922-925	PD3/2	CIE
573954	PD3/4	Northern General	581944	PD3/5	Leeds
573975-976	PD3/4	Northern General	581968-969	PD3/6	Bury
573977-978	PD3/4	Sunderland District	581998-999	PD3/5	Leeds
580209-212	PD3/4	Sunderland District	582000-002	PD3/5	Leeds
580227-228	PD3/6	Bury	582022-025	PD3/6	Bury
580232-234	PD3/6	Bury	582051-055	PD3/5	Leeds
580289-290	PD3/4	Sunderland District	582073-074	PD3/5	Leeds
580305-308	PD3/3	Western SMT	582099-101	PD3/5	Leeds
580331-334	PD3/3	Western SMT	582115-118	PD3/5	Leeds
580379-381	PD3/1	Scout, Preston	582209-211	PD3/4	Halifax
580401-404	PD3/3	Western SMT	582220	PD3/4	Halifax
580424-425	PD3/4	Sunderland District	582221	PD3/5	Leeds
580426-427	PD3/4	Gateshead & District	582251-253	PD3/5	Leeds
580451-455	PD3/6	Bury	582269-272	PD3/4	Halifax
580465-467	PD3/4	Gateshead & District	582276-277	PD3/6	Bury
580499-502	PD3/3	Western SMT	582292-293	PD3/6	Bury
580515-518	PD3/4	Tynemouth & District	582306-309	PD3/5	Leeds
580545-547	PD3/4	Tynemouth & District	582316-318	PD3/5	Leeds
580557-559	PD3/4	Tynemouth & District	582463-464	PD3/5	Leeds
580583	PD3/6	OK, Bishop Auckland	582470	PD3/5	Leeds
580584-585	PD3/3	Western SMT	582481-482	PD3/5	Leeds
580593-595	PD3/3	Western SMT	582518-521	PD3/2	CIE
580600-601	PD3/3	Western SMT	582522-524	PD3/5	Leeds
580632-635	PD3/4	Northern General	582541-545	PD3/4	Southdown
580641-644	PD3/4	Northern General	582563-567	PD3/4	Southdown
580659-664	PD3/1	Leicester	582581-585	PD3/4	Southdown
580723-724	PD3/4	Wakefields	582634	PD3/5	Leeds
580725-726	PD3/3	Western SMT	582658-659	PD3/5	Leeds
580740-744	PD3/4	Northern General	582663-665	PD3/5	Leeds
580782-785	PD3/4	Northern General	582676-683	PD3/2	CIE
580828-831	PD3/6	Southend	582704	PD3/5	Leeds
580854-855	PD3/3	Edinburgh	582748-749	PD3/3	South Notts, Gotham
580856	PD3/3	Western SMT	582764-768	PD3/1	Sheffield
580863-864	PD3/6	Southend	582787-788	PD3/6	Bury
580957	PD3/1	Skills, Nottingham	582797-799	PD3/6	Bury
580968-969	PD3/3	Western SMT	582835-839	PD3/1	Sheffield
580970-971	PD3/3	Edinburgh Corporation	582840	PD3/3	Baxter, Hanley
580972	PD3/3	Western SMT	582904	PD3/4	UTA
580998-999	PD3/3	Isle of Man Road Services	582976-979	PD3/5	Leeds
581000	PD3/3	Isle of Man Road Services	582996	PD3/3	Western SMT
581015-017	PD3/1	Leicester	583013-015	PD3/3	Western SMT
581024-026	PD3/1	Leicester	583078-080	PD3/5	Leeds
581141-144	PD3/3	Western SMT	583085-086	PD3/5	Leeds
581162-164	PD3/4	Northern General	583106-107	PD3/1	Sheffield
581165	PD3/5	Severn, Stainforth	583119-123	PD3/1	Sheffield
581182-184	PD3/4	Northern General	583132-135	PD3/2	CIE
581201-203	PD3/3	Western SMT	583138-140	PD3/1	Sheffield
581215-218	PD3/5	Preston	583251-255	PD3/5	Leeds
581224-226	PD3/5	Preston	583264	PD3/1	Delaine, Bourne
581281-283	PD3/3	Western SMT	583280-281	PD3/4	UTA

Chassis No	Model	Customer	Chassis No	Model	Customer
583294-298	PD3/5	Leeds	590408-409	PD3/1	Bournemouth
583302-306	PD3/5	Leeds	590484-487	PD3/2	CIE
583318-319	PD3/1	Sheffield	590577-578	PD3/2	Wigan
583320	PD3/5	Leeds	590584-587	PD3/2	CIE
583324-327	PD3/2	CIE	590594-596	PD3/2	Wigan
583328-332	PD3/1	Sheffield	590618-620	PD3/2	Wigan
583343-347	PD3/4	UTA	590630-631	PD3/2	Wigan
583364-366	PD3/1	Sheffield	590945	PD3/1	Delaine, Bourne
583401-403	PD3/4	UTA	591040-041	PD3/2	CIE
583432-433	PD3/4	UTA	591069-070	PD3/2	CIE
583447-450	PD3/4	Bolton	591249-256	PD3/2	CIE
583453	PD3/4	Bolton	591512	PD3/2	Millburn Motors, Glasgow
583479-483	PD3/3	Western SMT	591566-569	PD3/2	CIE
583494-498	PD3/3	Western SMT	591684	PD3/2	Millburn Motors, Glasgow
583512-513	PD3/4	UTA	591797-804	PD3/2	CIE
583517-518	PD3/3	Western SMT	591933-934	PD3/3	Western SMT
583521-524	PD3/3	Alexander	591951-952	PD3/3	Western SMT
583541	PD3/3	Alexander	591965-966	PD3/4	Southdown
583543-547	PD3/3	Western SMT	591977-978	PD3/4	Southdown
583559-563	PD3/3	Alexander	591993-994	PD3/3	Western SMT
583593-597	PD3/3	Western SMT	592001-002	PD3/3	Western SMT
583610-611	PD3/3	Western SMT	592009-011	PD3/3	Western SMT
583612-613	PD3/4	UTA	592041	PD3/3	Western SMT
583620-623	PD3/2	CIE	592042	PD3/4	Southdown
583637	PD3/4	UTA	592051-052	PD3/4	Southdown
583639	PD3/4	UTA	592061-062	PD3/4	Southdown
583660-664	PD3/3	Alexander	592078-079	PD3/4	Southdown
583693	PD3/1	Weardale Motor Services	592091-094	PD3/2	CIE
583700-701	PD3/3	Alexander	592097-098	PD3/4	Southdown
583717-718	PD3/5	Alexander	592109-110	PD3/3	Western SMT
583721-723	PD3/5	UTA	592140-141	PD3/4	Southdown
583729-731	PD3/2	CIE	592150-151	PD3/3	Western SMT
583732	PD3/1	Skills, Nottingham	592172-173	PD3/3	Western SMT
583733	PD3/3	Alexander	592180-181	PD3/4	Southdown
583761	PD3/3	Western SMT	592195-196	PD3/4	Southdown
583785	PD3/3	Western SMT	592208	PD3/4	Stratford Blue
583795	PD3/3	Western SMT	592229-230	PD3/4	Stratford Blue
583815	PD3/5	UTA	592245	PD3/4	Southdown
583831	PD3/1	Lloyd, Bagilt	592274-275	PD3/3	Western SMT
583907	PD3/5	UTA	592280-282	PD3/3	Western SMT
583917-924	PD3/2	CIE	592435-438	PD3/2	CIE
583939	PD3/6	Portsmouth	592671	PD3/1	AA, Ayr
583942	PD3/6	Portsmouth	592685	PD3/3	Alexander
583966-967	PD3/6	Portsmouth	592694-695	PD3/3	Alexander
583970	PD3/1	Turner, Brown Edge	592726-727	PD3/3	Alexander
583978	PD3/6	Portsmouth	592743	PD3/3	Alexander
590048-050	PD3/6	Western SMT	592755-756	PD3/1	Leicester
590052-059	PD3/3	Western SMT	592763-766	PD3/1	Leicester
590069	PD3/3	Western SMT	592797-798	PD3/1	Leicester
590070-071	PD3/6	Burnley, Colne & Nelson	592809-811	PD3/3	Alexander
590148-151	PD3/2	CIE	592822-823	PD3/1	South Yorkshire, Pontefract
590180-181	PD3/3	Western SMT	592851-852	PD3/3	Alexander
590184-185	PD3/3	Western SMT	592861	PD3/3	Alexander
590194-195	PD3/3	Western SMT	592862	PD3/1	Wallace Arnold
590203-204	PD3/3	Western SMT	592873-874	PD3/3	Alexander
590218-219	PD3/3	Western SMT	592924	PD3/3	Alexander
590266-267	PD3/1	Leicester	592981-983	PD3/3	Alexander
590272-273	PD3/1	Leicester	593083	PD3/3	Alexander
590278-279	PD3/1	Leicester	593108	PD3/3	Alexander
590352	PD3/1	Bournemouth	593110-111	PD3/2	Glasgow
590357-364	PD3/2	CIE	593177	PD3/2	Glasgow
590383-385	PD3/1	Bournemouth	600039-040	PD3/2	Glasgow
590388-389	PD3/1	Bournemouth	600042-043	PD3/2	Glasgow
590396-397	PD3/1	Bournemouth	600045-046	PD3/2	Glasgow

Chassis No	Model	Customer	Chassis No	Model	Customer
600049-050	PD3/2	Glasgow	601604-607	PD3/2	CIE
600053-054	PD3/2	Glasgow	601610-611	PD3/2	Glasgow
600057-058	PD3/2	Glasgow	601617-618	PD3/2	Glasgow
600098-099	PD3/2	Glasgow	601718-719	PD3/4	UTA
600108-109	PD3/2	Glasgow	601730	PD3A/2	Glasgow
600117-118	PD3/2	Glasgow	601756-758	PD3/1	Bournemouth
600127-128	PD3/2	Glasgow	601774	PD3/1	Bournemouth
600149-152	PD3/2	CIE	601788	PD3/1	Bournemouth
600223-224	PD3/2	Glasgow	601862-864	PD3/2	Glasgow
600233-234	PD3/2	Glasgow	601890-892	PD3/2	Wigan
600256-257	PD3/2	Glasgow	601904-905	PD3/2	Glasgow
600273-275	PD3/2	Glasgow	601907-908	PD3/4	UTA
600284-285	PD3/2	Glasgow	601915-922	PD3/2	CIE
600300-301	PD3/2	Glasgow	601927-929	PD3/2	Glasgow
600319-321	PD3/2	Glasgow	601943-944	PD3/4	UTA
600335-337	PD3/2	Glasgow	601954-956	PD3/2	Wigan
600349-350	PD3/2	Glasgow	601961-962	PD3/2	Glasgow
600395-396	PD3/4	UTA	601969-971	PD3/1	Bournemouth
600402-405	PD3/2	Glasgow	602000-001	PD3/2	Glasgow
600423-426	PD3/2	CIE	602013-014	PD3/4	UTA
600448-449	PD3/4	UTA	602025-026	PD3/4	UTA
600470-471	PD3/2	Glasgow	602027-029	PD3/2	Wigan
600478-479	PD3/2	Glasgow	602040-042	PD3/4	Southdown
600514-515	PD3/4	UTA	602063-065	PD3/2	Glasgow
600602-604	PD3/2	Glasgow	602085-087	PD3/4	Southdown
600626	PD3/2	Glasgow	602094-096	PD3/2	Wigan
600647-648	PD3/4	UTA	602119-122	PD3/4	Southdown
600649-651	PD3/2	Glasgow	602131-133	PD3/4	Southdown
600662	PD3/2	Glasgow	602141-142	PD3/2	Glasgow
600670-671	PD3/4	UTA	602143	PD3/4	Southdown
600710-711	PD3/2	Glasgow	602162-164	PD3/2	Glasgow
600722-725	PD3/2	CIE	602173-176	PD3/2	Glasgow
600827-828	PD3/2	Glasgow	602195-196	PD3/4	Southdown
600871-872	PD3/2	UTA	602209-210	PD3/4	Southdown
600896-899	PD3/2	Glasgow	602233-234	PD3/4	Southdown
600924-927	PD3/4	UTA	602249-250	PD3/4	Southdown
600935-938	PD3/2	UTA	602256-257	PD3/2	Glasgow
600953-956	PD3/4	Merthyr Tydfil	602264-267	PD3/2	CIE
600991-993	PD3/2	UTA	602268-269	PD3/4	Southdown
601011-012	PD3/4	UTA	602291-292	PD3/4	Southdown
601021-024	PD3/2	CIE	602301-302	PD3/4	Southdown
601093	PD3/2	Glasgow	602319-320	PD3/4	Southdown
601094-095	PD3/4	Merthyr Tydfil	602358-359	PD3/4	Southdown
601102-103	PD3/4	Merthyr Tydfil	602376-377	PD3/4	Southdown
601220-221	PD3/2	Glasgow	602403-410	PD3/5	Ashok Leyland
601232-233	PD3/2	Glasgow	602422-423	PD3/2	Glasgow
601234-235	PD3/4	UTA	602428-431	PD3/2	CIE
601308-311	PD3/2	CIE	602432-434	PD3/2	Glasgow
601332-333	PD3/4	Caerphilly	602474-476	PD3/4	Southdown
601341-344	PD3/4	UTA	602488-489	PD3/4	Southdown
601361-364	PD3/2	Glasgow	602509-510	PD3/4	Southdown
601375-376	PD3/2	Glasgow	602517-518	PD3/4	Southdown
601427-428	PD3/2	Glasgow	602534-537	PD3/5	Ashok Leyland
601444-445	PD3/4	UTA	602543-544	PD3/4	Southdown
601446	PD3/4	Southdown	602558-561	PD3/5	Ashok Leyland
601462-463	PD3/2	Glasgow	602584-585	PD3/4	Southdown
601495-496	PD3/2	Glasgow	602610-617	PD3/5	Ashok Leyland
601497	PD3/1	Bournemouth	602631-632	PD3/4	Southdown
601516	PD3/1	Bournemouth	602705-708	PD3/5	Ashok Leyland
601558-561	PD3/2	Glasgow	602793-800	PD3/2	CIE
601567-568	PD3/2	Glasgow	602936-937	PD3/4	Bolton
601576-577	PD3/2	Glasgow	602967-970	PD3/2	CIE
601578-579	PD3/4	UTA	602996-998	PD3/4	Bolton
601591-594	PD3/2	Glasgow	603003-005	PD3/4	Bolton

Chassis No	Model	Customer	Chassis No	Model	Customer
603023-030	PD3/5	Ashok Leyland	610456-457	PD3A/3	Western SMT
603043-045	PD3/4	Bolton	610460-462	PD3/4	UTA
603078-081	PD3/5	Ribble	610467-468	PD3/4	UTA
603092-097	PD3/5	Ashok Leyland	610486-490	PD3A/3	Western SMT
603106-108	PD3/5	Ribble	610551-553	PD3/4	UTA
603129-131	PD3/5	Ribble	610580-582	PD3/4	UTA
603149-151	PD3/5	Ribble	610602-603	PD3A/1	Leicester
603186-188	PD3/5	Ribble	610610-611	PD3A/3	Western SMT
603245-246	PD3/5	Ribble	610629-631	PD3A/1	Leicester
603255-262	PD3/3	Export	610652-654	PD3A/3	Western SMT
603263-264	PD3/5	Ribble	610769-771	PD3/4	UTA
603271	PD3/5	Ribble	610833-835	PD3A/3	Western SMT
603273-276	PD3/5	Ribble	610863-865	PD3/4	UTA
603295-299	PD3/2	CIE	610873-874	PD3A/2	Wigan
603310	PD3/5	Ribble	610921-923	PD3/4	UTA
603327-329	PD3/5	Ribble	610952-953	PD3/4	Severn, Stainforth
603347	PD3/5	Ribble	610991-992	PD3/4	UTA
603363	PD3/5	Ribble	610993-994	PD3/4	Merthyr Tydfil
603370-373	PD3/4	UTA	611028-030	PD3/4	Merthyr Tydfil
603374	PD3/5	Ribble	611096-098	PD3/5	Southdown
603382-386	PD3/5	Ribble	611115-117	PD3/4	Merthyr Tydfil
603392-394	PD3/5	Ribble	611132-134	PD3/5	Southdown
603396	PD3/5	Ribble	611146-147	PD3/5	Southdown
603399	PD3/5	Ribble	611158-160	PD3/5	Southdown
603412-415	PD3/3	Export	611174-176	PD3/5	Southdown
603416	PD3/5	Ribble	611183-186	PD3/5	Southdown
603418	PD3/5	Ribble	611200-202	PD3/5	Southdown
603463	PD3/4	UTA	611229-230	PD3/5	Southdown
603466-467	PD3/4	UTA	611248-249	PD3A/3	Western SMT
603473-474	PD3/5	Ribble	611274-276	PD3/5	Southdown
603496-497	PD3/5	Ribble	611322-325	PD3/4	Preston
603563	PD3/4	UTA	611329-332	PD3/5	Southdown
603589	PD3/4	UTA	611338-341	PD3/5	Southdown
603590-591	PD3/5	Ribble	611359-360	PD3/5	Southdown
603602	PD3/4	UTA	611373-374	PD3/5	Southdown
603611	PD3/6	Burnley, Colne & Nelson	611382-384	PD3/4	Preston
603614-615	PD3A/3	Western SMT	611410-412	PD3A/2	Huddersfield
610037-041	PD3A/3	Western SMT	611420-423	PD3A/2	Huddersfield
610042-043	PD3/4	UTA	611430-434	PD3A/2	Wigan
610044-048	PD3A/3	Alexander	611449-450	PD3A/1	Yorkshire Woollen
610053-058	PD3A/3	Western SMT	611451	PD3A/2	Huddersfield
610059-060	PD3/4	UTA	611460-461	PD3A/1	Yorkshire Woollen
610061-062	PD3A/3	Alexander	611465-466	PD3/5	Southdown
610092-093	PD3A/3	Alexander	611478-485	PD3/5	Ashok Leyland
610098-099	PD3/4	UTA	611535-536	PD3/4	Caerphilly
610127-128	PD3A/3	Western SMT	611565-567	PD3A/2	Wigan
610135-136	PD3/6	Burnley, Colne & Nelson	611576-579	PD3A/2	Wigan
610141-143	PD3A/1	Yorkshire Traction	611597-599	PD3A/1	Yorkshire Woollen
610149-151	PD3A/1	Yorkshire Traction	611650-657	PD3/5	Ashok Leyland
610152-153	PD3A/3	Western SMT	611804-811	PD3/5	Ashok Leyland
610177-179	PD3A/1	Yorkshire Traction	611875-876	PD3A/1	Yorkshire Woollen
610184-185	PD3A/1	Yorkshire Traction	611916-919	PD3/6	Export
610186-187	PD3A/3	Western SMT	611933-935	PD3A/2	Bolton
610222-225	PD3A/3	Alexander	611962-969	PD3/5	Ashok Leyland
610233-234	PD3/4	UTA	611980-982	PD3A/2	Bolton
610253-256	PD3A/3	Alexander	612030-032	PD3A/2	Bolton
610283-286	PD3A/3	Alexander	612059-062	PD3/6	Export
610313-315	PD3A/3	Western SMT	612071-073	PD3A/2	Bolton
610333-335	PD3A/3	Western SMT	612168-175	PD3/5	Ashok Leyland
610348-350	PD3A/3	Western SMT	612177-178	PD3A/2	Bolton
610351	PD3/6	South Notts	612199-201	PD3A/2	Bolton
610375-376	PD3A/3	Western SMT	612306-313	PD3/5	Ashok Leyland
610426-429	PD3A/3	Alexander	612367-370	PD3/5	Ribble
610437-439	PD3A/3	Western SMT	612379-380	PD3/5	Ribble

Chassis No	Model	Customer	Chassis No	Model	Customer
612388-391	PD3/5	Ashok Leyland	621066-073	PD3/5	Ashok Leyland
612392-393	PD3/5	Ribble	621182-191	PD3A/2	Leeds
612416-417	PD3/5	Ribble	621192-195	PD3/5	Ashok Leyland
612430-431	PD3/5	Ribble	621198-199	PD3/4	UTA
612446-447	PD3/5	Ribble	621237-238	PD3/4	UTA
612453-456	PD3/5	Ashok Leyland	621299-302	PD3/5	Ashok Leyland
612544-545	PD3/5	Ribble	621345	PD3A/2	Leyland-Albion (Africa)
612562-563	PD3A/1	Accrington	621349-350	PD3/4	UTA
612564-565	PD3/5	Ribble	621372-373	PD3/4	UTA
612573-576	PD3/5	Ashok Leyland	621418-419	PD3/4	UTA
612584-585	PD3/5	Ribble	621426-430	PD3/5	Ashok Leyland
612591-592	PD3/5	Ribble	621453-454	PD3/4	UTA
612615-616	PD3/5	Ribble	621571	PD3/4	Turner, Brown Edge
612635-637	PD3/5	Ribble	622039-041	PD3A/2	Huddersfield
612641-644	PD3/5	Ashok Leyland	622052-053	PD3A/2	Huddersfield
612665-666	PD3/5	Ribble	622070-072	PD3A/2	Huddersfield
612690-691	PD3/5	Ribble	622105-106	PD3A/2	Huddersfield
612701-709	PD3/5	Ashok Leyland	622402-407	PD3A/1	Cardiff
612757-758	PD3/5	Ribble	622493-496	PD3A/1	Leicester
612773-775	PD3/5	Ribble	622551-552	PD3A/1	Leicester
612782-783	PD3/5	Ribble	622559-560	PD3A/1	Leicester
612814-816	PD3/5	Ribble	622661-662	PD3A/1	Leicester
612844-847	PD3/5	Ribble	622754-757	PD3/6	Leyland-Albion (Africa)
613210	PD3A/1	Wallace Arnold	622876-879	PD3/6	Export
613396-398	PD3A/1	Yorkshire Traction	623029	PD3/5	Ribble
613515-517	PD3A/1	Yorkshire Traction	623149-152	PD3/6	Export
613555-556	PD3A/1	Yorkshire Traction	623209-213	PD3/6	Export
613596-599	PD3A/2	Export	623278-279	PD3/4	Stratford Blue
613611	PD3A/1	Yorkshire Traction	623354-356	PD3A/2	Huddersfield
613621-622	PD3A/1	Yorkshire Traction	623369-371	PD3A/2	Huddersfield
613695-696	PD3/4	UTA	623471-474	PD3/5	Leyland-Albion (Africa)
613706	PD3A/1	Yorkshire Traction	623510-513	PD3/5	Leyland-Albion (Africa)
620128	PD3/4	UTA	623593-594	PD3/4	Stratford Blue
620144-151	PD3/6	Export	623692-695	PD3/5	Leyland-Albion (Africa)
620171-172	PD3/4	UTA	623787-790	PD3/5	Leyland-Albion (Africa)
620181	PD3/4	UTA	623805-808	PD3A/1	Preston
620189-191	PD3A/2	Export	623861-864	PD3/5	Leyland-Albion (Africa)
620204	PD3/4	UTA	623877-879	PD3A/1	Preston
620241-244	PD3/5	Ashok Leyland	623992-996	PD3/5	Leyland-Albion (Africa)
620261-262	PD3/4	UTA	629038-041	PD3/4	Export
620263-264	PD3A/1	London Transport	629094	PD3/4	Caerphilly
620270-271	PD3/4	UTA	629105-108	PD3/4	Export
620319-320	PD3A/1	London Transport	629184-185	PD3/5	Ribble
620329-332	PD3/6	Export	629193-196	PD3/4	Export
620337-338	PD3/4	UTA	629199-201	PD3/5	Ribble
620380-385	PD3/6	Export	629240-241	PD3/5	Ribble
620387-388	PD3/4	UTA	629267-269	PD3/4	UTA
620443-444	PD3/4	UTA	629297-299	PD3/5	Ribble
620498-499	PD3A/1	Leigh	629316-318	PD3/4	UTA
620516-517	PD3A/1	Blackpool	629346	PD3A/1	Wallace Arnold
620535-536	PD3A/1	Blackpool	629364-366	PD3/5	Ribble
620562-563	PD3A/1	Blackpool	629378	PD3/5	Ribble
620592-593	PD3A/1	Blackpool	629404-407	PD3/4	Export
620614-615	PD3A/1	Blackpool	629422-423	PD3/5	Ribble
620652-653	PD3/4	UTA	629445-448	PD3/4	Export
620718-719	PD3A/1	Blackpool	629473	PD3/5	Ribble
620729-730	PD3/4	UTA	629532	PD3/5	Ribble
620748-749	PD3A/1	Blackpool	629538	PD3/5	Ribble
620804-805	PD3A/1	Blackpool	629552-559	PD3/4	Export
620845-846	PD3A/1	Blackpool	629656-662	PD3/4	Export
620876-877	PD3A/1	Blackpool	629757-758	PD3/5	Ribble
620922-923	PD3/4	UTA	L00029-030	PD3/5	Ribble
621016-019	PD3/4	Doncaster	L00034-045	PD3/5	Ribble
621043-053	PD3A/1	Leicester	L00220-226	PD3A/2	Leeds

Chassis No	Model	Customer	Chassis No	Model	Customer
L00372-375	PD3/5	Leyland-Albion (Africa)	L03531-538	PD3/5	Leyland-Albion (Africa)
L00441-444	PD3/5	Leyland-Albion (Africa)	L03582-589	PD3/5	Leyland-Albion (Africa)
L00470-473	PD3A/1	London Transport	L03590-593	PD3/4	Southdown
L00706	PD3A/1	Accrington	L03662-671	PD3/5	Leyland-Albion (Africa)
L00707	PD3/4	Severn, Stainforth	L03712-716	PD3A/1	Yorkshire Traction
L00718-720	PD3A/2	Leeds	L03887-888	PD3A/2	Export
L00724-731	PD3/5	Leyland-Albion (Africa)	L04016-020	PD3A/1	Yorkshire Traction
L00831-839	PD3/5	Leyland-Albion (Africa)	L04054-055	PD3A/1	Yorkshire Traction
L01321-324	PD3A/1	Bournemouth	L04114-117	PD3/4	Merthyr Tydfil
L01366-369	PD3/4	Halifax	L04407-410	PD3/4	Rawtenstall
L01401-404	PD3/5	Leyland-Albion (Africa)	L20001-002	PD3A/1	Darwen
L01405-408	PD3A/1	Bournemouth	L20075	PD3/4	Severn, Stainforth
L01421-424	PD3/4	Halifax	L20143-147	PD3/5	Oldham
L01431	PD3A/2	Export	L20237-241	PD3/5	Oldham
L01484-488	PD3/5	Leyland-Albion (Africa)	L20346-347	PD3A/1	Preston
L01493-494	PD3A/1	Bournemouth	L20641-643	PD3A/1	Preston
L01532-535	PD3/5	Leyland-Albion (Africa)	L20653-655	PD3/6	Isle of Man Road Services
L01628-635	PD3/5	Leyland-Albion (Africa)	L20692-693	PD3A/1	Leicester
L01646-648	PD3/4	Doncaster	L20797	PD3/4	Clark & Rose, Aberdeen
L01668-671	PD3A/1	Blackpool	L20819-820	PD3/6	Edinburgh
L01693-695	PD3/4	Doncaster	L20856-857	PD3A/1	Leicester
L01700-701	PD3A/1	Blackpool	L20877-878	PD3A/1	Leicester
L01726-730	PD3/5	Leyland-Albion (Africa)	L20903-904	PD3/6	Edinburgh
L01754-755	PD3A/1	Blackpool	L20905-908	PD3A/1	Leicester
L01776-777	PD3A/1	Blackpool	L20975-978	PD3/6	Edinburgh
L01949-950	PD3A/2	Accrington	L21051-054	PD3/6	Edinburgh
L02388-395	PD3/4	Export	L21143-146	PD3/6	Edinburgh
L02410-412	PD3A/1	Leicester	L21247-250	PD3/6	Edinburgh
L02461-464	PD3/4	Export	L21305-308	PD3/6	Edinburgh
L02477-482	PD3A/1	Stratford Blue	L21455-456	PD3/6	Edinburgh
L02483-485	PD3/4	Southdown	L21469-470	PD3/6	Edinburgh
L02493-494	PD3/4	Southdown	L21515-518	PD3/6	Edinburgh
L02495-496	PD3A/1	County Motors, Lepton	L21616-617	PD3/6	Edinburgh
L02527-530	PD3/4	Export	L21663-664	PD3/6	Edinburgh
L02533-537	PD3/4	Southdown	L21690-691	PD3/6	Edinburgh
L02551-553	PD3/4	Southdown	L21752-753	PD3/6	Edinburgh
L02585-588	PD3/4	Southdown	L21899	PD3/6	Edinburgh
L02592-595	PD3A/1	Leicester	L22020-022	PD3/6	Edinburgh
L02596-598	PD3/4	Southdown	L22085-086	PD3/6	Edinburgh
L02621-622	PD3/4	Southdown	L22110	PD3/6	Edinburgh
L02635-638	PD3/4	Export	L22152-154	PD3/6	Edinburgh
L02660-661	PD3A/1	Leicester	L22415-418	PD3/5	Cape Tramways
L02690-693	PD3/5	Leyland-Albion (Africa)	L22427-430	PD3/5	Cape Tramways
L02760-767	PD3/5	Leyland-Albion (Africa)	L22541-552	PD3/5	Cape Tramways
L02785-786	PD3A/1	Leicester	L22814-818	PD3/5	Cape Tramways
L02864-866	PD3/4	Southdown	L22967-968	PD3/4	Southdown
L02913-914	PD3A/1	Leicester	L23475-476	PD3/4	Southdown
L02928-935	PD3/4	Export	L23486-487	PD3/4	Southdown
L02938-939	PD3/4	Southdown	L23539-540	PD3/4	Southdown
L02940-941	PD3A/1	Leicester	L23566-567	PD3/4	Southdown
L02996-998	PD3/4	Southdown	L23678-680	PD3/4	Southdown
L03018-019	PD3A/1	Leicester	L23711-712	PD3/6	Southend
L03038-041	PD3/5	Leyland-Albion (Africa)	L23728-729	PD3/6	Southend
L03042-045	PD3/5	Leyland-Albion (Africa)	L23738-739	PD3/4	Southdown
L02054-056	PD3A/1	Leicester	L23782-783	PD3/6	Southend
L03146-148	PD3/4	Southdown	L23794-797	PD3/4	Southdown
L03195-202	PD3/5	Leyland-Albion (Africa)	L23815-816	PD3/6	Southend
L03224-226	PD3/4	Southdown	L23847-848	PD3/4	Southdown
L03262	PD3/4	Southdown	L23883-886	PD3/6	Southend
L03269-276	PD3/5	Leyland-Albion (Africa)	L23973-974	PD3/4	Southdown
L03366-368	PD3/4	Southdown	L23993-995	PD3A/1	Yorkshire Traction
L03397-398	PD3/4	Southdown	L24026-028	PD3/4	Southdown
L03452-459	PD3/5	Leyland-Albion (Africa)	L24029-032	PD3A/1	Yorkshire Traction
L03502-505	PD3/4	Southdown	L24084-086	PD3A/1	Yorkshire Traction

Chassis No	Model	Customer	Chassis No	Model	Customer
L24152-153	PD3/4	Southdown	L60140-141	PD3A/1	Leicester
L24333-340	PD3/4	Ashok Leyland	L60163-165	PD3/4	Southdown
L24401-402	PD3/4	Southdown	L60225-226	PD3A/	Wallace Arnold
L24417-418	PD3/4	Southdown	L60373-374	PD3A/1	Leicester
L24481-482	PD3/4	Southdown	L60452-453	PD3/4	Southdown
L24454-461	PD3/5	Cape Tramways	L60463	PD3/4	Southdown
L24493-494	PD3/4	Southdown	L60487-488	PD3A/2	Edinburgh
L24558-561	PD3/4	Ashok Leyland	L60581-582	PD3A/2	Edinburgh
L24599-600	PD3A/1	Blackpool	L60635	PD3/4	Merthyr Tydfil
L24605-608	PD3/4	Southdown	L60644	PD3A/1	Leicester
L24673-675	PD3A/1	Blackpool	L60656-657	PD3/4	Southdown
L24676	PD3A/1	Ramsbottom	L60721-722	PD3A/2	Edinburgh
L24688-691	PD3/4	Ashok Leyland	L60981-983	PD3A/2	Edinburgh
L24716-717	PD3A/1	Blackpool	L61079	PD3A/1	Leicester
L24741-744	PD3/4	Ashok Leyland	L61095-097	PD3A/2	Edinburgh
L24797-799	PD3A/1	Blackpool	L61196-198	PD3A/2	Edinburgh
L24900-902	PD3A/1	Blackpool	L61283	PD3A/1	Leicester
L24923-926	PD3/5	Leyland-Albion (Africa)	L61291	PD3/4	Southdown
L24937-939	PD3A/1	Blackpool	L61304-305	PD3A/2	Edinburgh
L24964-967	PD3/5	Leyland-Albion (Africa)	L61391	PD3A/1	Leicester
L24976-979	PD3/4	Ashok Leyland	L61394-400	PD3A/1	Leicester
L25016-017	PD3A/1	Blackpool	L61414-415	PD3A/2	Edinburgh
L25068-069	PD3A/1	Blackpool	L61529	PD3/4	Southdown
L25119-122	PD3/5	Ashok Leyland	L61536-537	PD3A/2	Edinburgh
L25149-150	PD3/4	Ramsbottom	L61543-544	PD3/4	Southdown
L40008-015	PD3/4	Ashok Leyland	L61720-721	PD3A/2	Edinburgh
L40119	PD3/4	Rawtenstall	L61728-729	PD3/4	Southdown
L40173-176	PD3/5	Leyland-Albion (Africa)	L61822-823	PD3A/2	Edinburgh
L40183-186	PD3/4	Ashok Leyland	L61901-902	PD3/4	Southdown
L40247-250	PD3/5	Ashok Leyland	L61944-945	PD3/4	Southdown
L40271-275	PD3/5	Leyland-Albion (Africa)	L62114-116	PD3/4	Southdown
L40352-354	PD3A/	Darwen	L62180-181	PD3/4	Southdown
L40483-486	PD3/5	Ashok Leyland	L62201	PD3/4	Haslingden
L40561-568	PD3/4	Ashok Leyland	L62399-400	PD3/4	Rawtenstall
L40652-655	PD3/5	Ashok Leyland	L62412-413	PD3/4	Rawtenstall
L40755-757	PD3/4	Merthyr Tydfil	L62503	PD3/4	Merthyr Tydfil
L40821-828	PD3/5	Leyland-Albion (Africa)	L62519-520	PD3/4	Brighton
L40996-999	PD3/5	Ashok Leyland	L62736	PD3/4	Brighton
L41053-060	PD3/5	Leyland-Albion (Africa)	L62742	PD3/4	Merthyr Tydfil
L41086-093	PD3/4	Ashok Leyland	L62743	PD3/4	Brighton
L41171-174	PD3/5	Ashok Leyland	L62846-847	PD3/4	Merthyr Tydfil
L41278-281	PD3/4	Ashok Leyland	L62870	PD3/4	Brighton
L41406-409	PD3/4	Ashok Leyland	L63130-144	PD3A/2	Bradford
L41511-513	PD3/4	Ashok Leyland	L63569	PD3/4	Forbes, Aberdeen
L41514-517	PD3/5	Leyland-Albion (Africa)	L63673	PD3/4	Southdown
L41605-608	PD3/5	Ashok Leyland	L63881	PD3/4	Southdown
L41705-706	PD3A/1	Wallace Arnold	L63895-896	PD3/4	Southdown
L41709	PD3/4	Rawtenstall	L63987-989	PD3/4	Southdown
L41740-743	PD3/5	Leyland-Albion (Africa)	L64108-110	PD3/4	Southdown
L41776-779	PD3/5	Ashok Leyland	L64215-216	PD3/4	Southdown
L41934-938	PD3/5	Ashok Leyland	L64340-341	PD3/4	Southdown
L42185-188	PD3/5	Leyland-Albion (Africa)	L64455-456	PD3/4	Southdown
L42422	PD3/4	Caerphilly	L64673-674	PD3A/1	Blackpool
L42432-435	PD3/5	Ashok Leyland	L64686-687	PD3/4	Southdown
L42563-570	PD3/5	Leyland-Albion (Africa)	L64702-703	PD3A/1	Blackpool
L42817-818	PD3/4	Caerphilly	L64944-945	PD3/4	Southdown
L42961	PD3A/1	London Transport	L65087-090	PD3/4	Southdown
L43176-177	PD3A/1	Stratford Blue	L65207-208	PD3A/2	Accrington
L44505	PD3A/1	Ramsbottom	L65362-363	PD3A/2	Accrington
L44813-814	PD3A/1	Leicester	700133-137	PD3A/1	Blackpool
L45031-033	PD3/4	Southdown	700252-253	PD3A/1	Blackpool
L45042-044	PD3A/1	Leicester	700322-324	PD3A/1	Blackpool
L45054-056	PD3/4	Southdown	700338	Spl	Ashok Leyland
L45150-151	PD3/4	Southdown	700490-492	PD3A/1	Blackpool

Chassis No	Model	Customer	Chassis No	Model	Customer
700589-591	PD3A/1	Blackpool	703413	PD3/4	Clark & Rose, Aberdeen
700616-617	PD3A/1	Blackpool	703414	PD3/A12	Bradford
700827-828	PD3A/1	Blackpool	703462-469	PD3/Spl	Ashok Leyland
700851	PD3A/1	Blackpool	703488-489	PD3/14	Stockport
700887-890	PD3/15	Export	703501-502	PD3A/12	Bradford
701047-050	PD3/15	Export	703569-570	PD3A/12	Bradford
701164-167	PD3/15	Export	703581-592	PD3/Spl	Ashok Leyland
701219-220	PD3/4	Ramsbottom	703596-597	PD3/14	Stockport
701311-314	PD3/15	Export	703634-635	PD3/14	Stockport
701355-356	PD3A/12	Leicester	703728-739	PD3/Spl	Ashok Leyland
701426-428	PD3/Spl	Ashok Leyland	703742-743	PD3/14	Stockport
701459-462	PD3/15	Export	703860-871	PD3/Spl	Ashok Leyland
701633-636	PD3/15	Export	703962-973	PD3/Spl	Ashok Leyland
701732-743	PD3/15	Export	703981	PD3/4	Bedwas & Machen
701802	PD3/14	Haslingden	800015-024	PD3/Spl	Ashok Leyland
701824-835	PD3/15	Export	800113-120	PD3/Spl	Ashok Leyland
701871-872	PD3A/12	Leicester	800196-203	PD3/Spl	Ashok Leyland
701890-891	PD3A/12	Leicester	800478-479	PD3/11	Blackpool
701926-927	PD3A/1	Harper, Heath Hayes	800551-558	PD3/Spl	Ashok Leyland
701948-959	PD3/15	Export	800591-592	PD3/11	Blackpool
702060-075	PD3/15	Export	800677-684	PD3/Spl	Ashok Leyland
702136-137	PD3A/12	Leicester	800706-707	PD3/11	Blackpool
702270-272	PD3A/12	Leicester	800836-837	PD3/11	Blackpool
702346-347	PD3A/12	Leicester	800994-995	PD3/11	Blackpool
702350-351	PD3/4	Ramsbottom	801069-070	PD3/Spl	Ashok Leyland
702607-608	PD3A/12	Leicester	801090-091	PD3/11	Blackpool
702609	PD3/4	Southend	801237-239	PD3/11	Blackpool
702662-663	PD3A/12	Leicester	801752	PD3A/2	Harper, Heath Hayes
702664-665	PD3/4	Southend	802657	PD3/11	Export (Indonesia)
702710-712	PD3A/12	Leicester	803897-898	PD3/14	Stockport
702825	PD3/14	Stockport	803941-942	PD3/14	Stockport
702872	PD3A/12	Bradford	804002-003	PD3/14	Stockport
702948-949	PDA3/12	Bradford	804344-347	PD3/14	Stockport
702980-981	PD3A/12	Bradford	804370-371	PD3/14	Stockport
703033	PD3A/12	Bradford	804987	PD3/14	Ramsbottom
703083-084	PD3/14	Stockport	902844	PD3/14	Ramsbottom
703133-134	PD3A/12	Bradford	7002624-631	PD3/Spl	Ashok Leyland
703194-195	PD3/14	Stockport	7002928-937	PD3/Spl	Ashok Leyland
703299-300	PD3A/12	Bradford	7003154-161	PD3/Spl	Ashok Leyland
703394-395	PD3/14	Stockport	7003746-749	PD3/Spl	Ashok Leyland

Appendix 2:
Albion Lowlander Chassis List

Albion's chassis numbering system used a series of suffix letters, from A to F, followed by H and then J to L, giving groups of 10 chassis with the same number but different suffix letters, as the list below shows. The letters G and I were excluded because of possible confusion with the figures 6 and 1.

Chassis No	Model	Customer	Chassis No	Model	Customer
62100A-B	LR1	Western SMT	62111K-L	LR1	Western SMT
62100C	LR1	Demonstrator	62112A-E	LR1	Western SMT
62100D	LR1	Edinburgh	62112F	LR3	South Notts
62100E	LR1	Central SMT	62112H-L	LR1	Western SMT
62100F	LR1	Western SMT	62113A-L	LR1	Western SMT
62100H	LR7	East Midland	62114A-C	LR1	Western SMT
62100J	LR1	Western SMT	62114D-L	LR7	Luton
62100K-L	LR1	Central SMT	62115A	LR1	Western SMT
62101A-B	LR1	Western SMT	62115B-F	LR1	Alexander (Midland)
62101C-D	LR1	Central SMT	62115H-L	LR1	Central SMT
62101E	LR1	Alexander (Midland)	62116A	LR1	Central SMT
62101F-J	LR1	Western SMT	62116B-F	LR1	Alexander (Midland)
62101K	LR1	Central SMT	62116H-K	LR1	Central SMT
62101L	LR1	Western SMT	62116L	LR1	Western SMT
62102A-D	LR1	Central SMT	62117A-F	LR1	Western SMT
62102E-F	LR1	Western SMT	62117H-K	LR1	Alexander (Midland)
62102H-L	LR1	Alexander (Midland)	62117L	LR1	Central SMT
62103A-C	LR1	Alexander (Midland)	62118A-B	LR1	Central SMT
62103D-L	LR1	Alexander (Fife)	62118C-D	LR1	Alexander (Midland)
62104A-D	LR1	Alexander (Midland)	62118E-F	LR1	Central SMT
62104E-L	LR1	Western SMT	62118H-K	LR1	Alexander (Midland)
62105A-C	LR1	Western SMT	62118L	LR1	Central SMT
62105D	LR1	Alexander (Midland)	62119A-B	LR1	Central SMT
62105E-L	LR1	Western SMT	62119C-D	LR1	Western SMT
62106A	LR1	Western SMT	62119E-H	LR1	Central SMT
62106B-H	LR1	Alexander (Midland)	62119J-K	LR1	Western SMT
62106J	LR7	Luton	62119L	LR1	Central SMT
62106K	LR1	Western SMT	62120A-L	LR1	Western SMT
62106L	LR7	East Midland	62121A-L	LR1	Western SMT
62107A-E	LR7	East Midland	62122A-D	LR1	Western SMT
62107F-H	LR7	Luton	62122E-L	LR7	Yorkshire Woollen
62107J-L	LR7	East Midland	62123A-J	LR7	Yorkshire Woollen
62108A-D	LR7	East Midland	62123K-L	LR1	Ribble
62108E	LR1	Alexander (Midland)	62124A-E	LR1	Ribble
62108F-J	LR7	Luton	62124F	LR3	South Notts
62108K-L	LR7	Southend	62124H-K	LR1	Ribble
62109A-J	LR7	Southend	62124L	LR7	Western SMT
62109K-L	LR7	Luton	62125A-L	LR7	Western SMT
62110A	LR7	Luton	62126A	LR7	Western SMT
62110B-F	LR1	Western SMT	62126B	LR3	South Notts
62110H-K	LR1	Alexander (Midland)	62126C-J	LR1	Ribble
62110L	LR1	Western SMT	62126K	LR3	South Notts
62111A-C	LR1	Western SMT	62126L	LR7	East Midland
62111D-F	LR1	Alexander (Midland)	62127A-C	LR7	East Midland
62111H-J	LR1	Alexander (Northern)	62127D	LR3	South Notts